P9-DFL-386

WORDS OF WISDOM FROM GUY WRITERS

"A lot of guys I know like to read and write violent stuff. And I think it's because guys are always testing themselves. They want to see what they can do. They want some action. They want something real."

—JON SCIESZKA, author of the Time Warp Trio series

"One of my favorite superheroes is Spider-Man, a classic example of a flawed hero. You gotta feel for a guy who can bench-press a bus but can't talk to the girl."

—GREG TRINE, author of the
Melvin Beederman, Superhero series

"I'd rather leave the house naked than without a pen and my little notebook."

—ROBERT LIPSYTE, bestselling author of
The Contender and *Center Field*

"I read constantly in the realms of history, folklore, legend, myths, ghostlores, and other paranormal events. I keep what I call a 'Weird File' of newspaper clippings. . . . You just never know where ideas will come from."

—ROBERT D. SAN SOUCI, author of *Haunted Houses*

"I got in trouble a few times in high school because I was passing around my cartoons during class. . . . Lucky for me, when I got caught, I was given the job as cartoonist for the school newspaper."

—JARRETT J. KROSOCZKA, author of the Lunch Lady series

GUY-WRITE

GUY-WRITE

WHAT EVERY GUY WRITER NEEDS TO KNOW

Ralph Fletcher

Christy Ottaviano Books
Henry Holt and Company   New York

ACKNOWLEDGMENTS

Since professional writers are incredibly busy, I am incredibly grateful to the ones who took time from their busy schedules to let me interview them for this book: Jarrett Krosoczka, Robert Lipsyte, Robert San Souci, Jon Scieszka, Greg Trine, and Jane Yolen.

Mega thanks to the kids who let me use their drawings in this book: Adam Bissonette, Santiago Cursi-Fletcher, Joseph Fletcher, Robert Fletcher, Shane Maxwell, and Francis Ohe.

Thanks also to the guys whose writing appears in this book: Ben Allen, Adam Bissonette, Taylor Curtis, Brandon Dunham, Joseph Fletcher, Robert Fletcher, Max Friedman, Max Gilmore, Jimmy Hernandez, Kenny Le, Alex Lemus, Zack Smith, and Ben Whea.

I know many teachers who are working hard to widen the circle for boy writers, including Jen Allen, Chris Boydstun, Jody Chang, Paul Crivelli, Bob Crongeyer, Jeremy Hyler, Kate Morris, and Erin McIntyre. Thanks to Linda Rief and Suzanne Whaley. And finally, I'm grateful to my wonderful wife, JoAnn, for nurturing all the guy writers, young and old, in our family.

Henry Holt and Company, LLC
Publishers since 1866
175 Fifth Avenue
New York, New York 10010
mackids.com

Henry Holt® is a registered trademark of Henry Holt
and Company, LLC.
Copyright © 2012 by Ralph Fletcher
All rights reserved.

Library of Congress Cataloging-in-Publication Data
Fletcher, Ralph J.
Guy-write : what every guy writer needs to know /
by Ralph Fletcher. — 1st ed.
p.   cm.
Includes index.
ISBN 978-0-8050-9404-6 (hc)
1. Children's literature—Authorship—Juvenile
literature.   2. Authorship—Juvenile literature.
3. Authors—Juvenile literature.   4. Illustrators—
Juvenile literature.   I. Title.
PN147.5.F57 2012   808.06'8—dc23   2011033487

First Edition—2012 / Design by Meredith Pratt
Printed in the United States of America by
R. R. Donnelley & Sons Company, Harrisonburg, Virginia

1 3 5 7 9 10 8 6 4 2

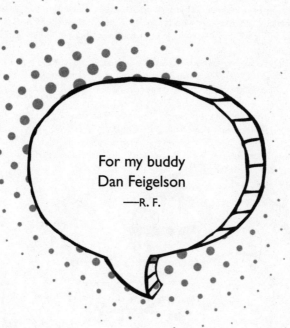

For my buddy
Dan Feigelson
——R. F.

CONTENTS

Dude, You
Are Not Alone

few years ago we took our kids to Lubec, Maine,
where we have a camp on a tidal river. At ten p.m.
on a clear autumn night, my sixteen-year-old son, Robert,
was sitting by a campfire near the water's edge with two
of his buddies Thomas and Greg. When I happened to
walk nearby, I expected to find them yukking it up, so I
was surprised to hear nothing but the crackling flames. I
saw that each of them had directed a flashlight beam
down at a book splayed open on his lap. What were they
doing? Moving closer, I could see that the books were
notebooks.

They were writing. On a beautiful September evening,
those guys spent almost an hour writing quietly in their
notebooks.

Some people consider writing to be little more than
boring nerd work. Wrong! Written words pack a punch.
If you ask a question you might get blown off, but it's a lot

less likely you'll get ignored (by a teacher or a girl you like) when you put questions or thoughts in writing. Writing demands a reaction—and usually gets it.

But writing is not just about power; it's about fun. Lately I've been working on a collection of Pointless Stories. This morning I was writing one titled "The Boy Who Swallowed a Parenthesis." The main character is a kid named Bobb-With-Two-B's Barnwell. Sure, it's a goofy idea, but I'm having a blast writing it. Who cares if it ever gets published? I'm doing it for me.

If you're like most guys, you actually do like to write, even if you don't advertise this fact. You enjoy how it feels to create a potion of words, drawings, and symbols. You love letting your imagination romp like a wild stallion in whatever direction it wants. You have favorite tools—a laptop, notebook, sketchbook, favorite pen—and maybe even your own "writing place."

So far so good. But in school certain things conspire to dampen your enthusiasm:

You almost **never** get a chance to do any freewriting.

When you try to take your own unique approach to an assigned topic, **your teacher doesn't appreciate it.**

You write one of your best papers, but the teacher gives you a **mediocre grade.**

Your handwriting resembles the **nervous scratchings** made by chickens and guinea hens when hungry foxes prowl nearby.

You get marked down for spelling and punctuation.

For many guys, school writing can really stink. A fifth-grader named Brandon explained it to me like this:

> In school we always have to write nonfiction, realistic stuff like what really happened. We aren't allowed to include guns—not even if the character is a policeman. I wish we could write about what we really think and feel. I wish we could write things like real hard fiction with people dropping from helicopters, maybe a baby being carried away and tipping off a cliff, hitting a chipmunk. There is no actual fiction in school. We always have to make it like a true story.

Does any of this ring true? If it does, take heart. Although you may feel isolated, you're not alone. I have surveyed guys around the country, and many feel the same. They feel that too many teachers simply don't get the writing of boys.

One area where boy writers consistently get shot down in school is when they attempt to include violence, weapons, or warfare in their writing. (I explore this idea in chapter 4.) In Michigan I met a first-grader named Steven who had written a poem he was eager to share with me.

Weed Hunter

I feel like I am hunting a very victorious plant, a weed.
I circle it. I study it. I watch its every move.
I always take it by the roots.

My weapon is a shovel.

Weeds come up way ahead of the other plants.

I shall pull up every one I see and
put it in a very dry place without any dirt.

I will defeat these weeds
even if it will take my entire life!

I liked Steven's poem. Wait, strike that—I LOVED it! Six years old, and this kid is already a strong writer. Steven was proud of his weed poem. He looked forward to having it published in the class anthology and sharing it at the author's celebration being held at his school.

But because of one word, Steven's poem was not allowed to be displayed on the wall or included in the class anthology. Can you find that dangerous, dreadful, despicable word? (Hint: Check the fourth line.)

Weapon.

Steven's school had a no-tolerance policy regarding violence and weapons. That's fine, but in this case the policy was enforced so rigidly that even the written word *weapon* was considered too dangerous and had to be banned.

Hel-lo?

When I first heard about what happened to Steven and his weed poem, I wanted to burst out laughing, except I quickly realized it isn't funny. It's tragic. The result: one more boy writer censored and silenced.

Many guys like to take chances. It's part of our DNA. But often when guys take chances in their writing and push the limits of what is allowed in school—WHAM!— they run into a buzz saw and get knocked down by the powers that be.

But take heart, my fellow word-warriors. We have lost some battles, but the war is not over. Reinforcements are coming. A movement has sprung up aimed at appreciating guys as writers and as readers, and I'm proud to be part of that movement. We're working hard to revamp classrooms in order to make them friendlier to the kind of topics guys like to write about, and the ways we like to express ourselves on paper. A number of factors have gone into the creation of some positive changes, including

- Teachers (many female teachers, in fact) who have created **"boy writing clubs"** where guys can write for fun, celebrate each other's writing, and not get into trouble for including a fart in a story.

- Authors like Jon Scieszka (who wrote <u>The Stinky Cheese Man</u>) who have created articles, Web sites, and films aimed at **widening the circle** for guy writers.

- Many important new books are being published by experts who argue that **schools must become friendlier to guy writers and readers.** I published my own book titled <u>Boy Writers: Reclaiming Their Voices</u>. Today I speak about this subject at conferences around the country and abroad. Here's the good news: 99 percent of the teachers I speak to are receptive to this idea. They know that guy writers really do have important things to say and teachers have to do a better job of reaching out to guys. Yes, it will take time, but things are beginning to change.

Have you ever picked up a baseball and really studied it? An official baseball has exactly 108 double stitches. The "sweet spot" on a baseball is located on the area of leather directly between the stitched seams. Well, there's a sweet spot in writing, too. Before I tell you what it is, I'll say what it's NOT—it's not writing for punishment, not doing formulaic writing or five-paragraph essays, and definitely not stick-to-the-prompt test practice (ugh).

The sweet spot in writing is when you're so totally involved in what you're writing that you lose track of time and forget where you are. I know when my sons have found their sweet spot because they're writing fast and loose, maybe IM'ing on the computer or scribbling in a notebook, laughing, reading out loud, sharing with each other or with someone online, or maybe so focused they're oblivious to everything around them. It's when you're so lost writing a story about a hot summer day that you get surprised when you look up and see snow falling outside your window.

I've published forty-one books, and I'm not done yet. I wrote this book to help guys who want to become better writers. The stronger you are as a writer, the more you'll enjoy it. Earning a high grade for an essay is wonderful. It's a kick to get a poem or story published in a magazine or online site. But those are external rewards. I'm more interested in the *inside* game of writing. My purpose isn't so much to help you with your school writing (although it may) but to help you with the real writing you do when you're locked in, lost in your imagination, when you're mixing words and sentences like some kind of mad scientist or word architect trying to construct a city of words.

I'll talk about the kinds of things guys typically like to write about: spoofs, humor, sports, blood, farts, giant monsters tearing down the city, and a few serious subjects, too. You'll find lots of examples from young writers and lots of drawings from guy writers like yourselves. In most cases these drawings came from their writing notebooks. Creating these drawings helped these writers tell the story they wanted to tell. You'll also find interviews with a few guy writers whose books you might have read (or at least heard of). Each chapter includes practical advice, tips, and strategies designed to help you lift your writing to the next level so you can grow into the kind of writer you want to be.

Humor

Okay, everyone has heard of North Face gear, but have you heard about a clothing line named the South Butt? Their products include the South Butt "Little Pooper" series for toddlers, and the South Butt Butt Pack. This line of apparel was started by a teenager named Jimmy Winkelmann, a guy who wanted to poke fun at people who, he believed, bought the North

Face brand as a status symbol even though they weren't really interested in the outdoors. The North Face slogan is "Never Stop Exploring." By contrast, Winkelmann created "Never Stop Relaxing" as the slogan for the South Butt.

This is an example of spoof, satire, or parody, a form of writing that most guys adore. Writing a satire/parody isn't very complicated. To do so, you simply take a familiar form or genre and then change it in some way. This creates the humor.

Take, for example, my teenage son Joseph. For as long as I can remember, Joseph has written a Christmas letter to Santa Claus. These letters were very sincere when he was a little boy, but as he grew older I noticed that they began to change. Joseph's Santa letters became funnier, if not as sweet. Here's a Santa letter Joseph wrote when he was in seventh grade.

Dear Santa,

   Now, I know I haven't been perfect this year, but let's be real, I mean who has? And plus, I have been doing much better in school this year so I'll take my chances and ask for what this kid REALLY wants and hope for the better.

I would like for Christmas (listed from most desired to least desired):

1. An Xbox 360 with hard drive and wireless controller (see my big brother Adam, he'll know which one I'm looking for)

Just in case I get anything else after this wallet-emptier, I'll continue . . .

2. "A Long Story Short" ski video (purchasable from level1productions.com)

3. A piano book of songs that I like and would enjoy playing

These are the three main things I'm asking for. As for anything else, surprise me ☺.

Sincerely yours,

Joseph Fletcher

This letter is half serious, half spoof. On one hand, Joseph really does want to tell "Santa" what he wants. But at the same time, he's taken the traditional form of a letter to Santa and twisted it by including some irreverent humor (*wallet-emptier*, for instance) that makes me laugh. It's fun to read.

I know a fifth-grader named Johnny. He wanted to describe a pumpkin at Halloween, but he knew for sure he didn't want to write another jolly jack-o'-lantern story. Here's what Johnny came up with.

Pumpkin

*I love your uneven eyes. How
can I forget your rotten teeth?
His teeth are so rotten they have
holes in them . . .*

*. . . because he doesn't brush his
teeth. You have to get your teeth
done. Can you please leave the room,
Pumpkin?*

*I'm going to have to talk silently
because he listens to all my conversations.
But he's actually crazy! So take caution.*

*Never trust him or play Monopoly
with him because he has a low
self of steem.*

Love it! Even the "mistake" (*self of steem*) in the last line is flat-out hilarious. I love the way Johnny alternates between talking to the pumpkin and then whispering side comments about the pumpkin to the reader. By infusing a dose of dark humor, Johnny transformed what could have been a dull topic into something strong and memorable.

In my own writing I have learned and relearned how important it is to include humor. Readers will follow you anywhere if you can make them laugh. I try hard to weave in events, characters, or dialogue that will do just that. My book *Uncle Daddy* is a serious novel. But I knew readers would also want some comic relief, so I created a character named Ethan Pierce, an annoying kid who has some of the best (and funniest) lines in the book. In my novel *Spider Boy*, Bobby borrows some pig eyeballs from the school science lab and brings them home. When his sister's boyfriend comes to the house for supper, Bobby deliberately hides the pig eyeballs in a bowl of olives. You can imagine the uproar that results when someone reaches into the olive bowl.

I'm always on the lookout for potentially funny material in my own life that could liven up a book. (Once, during a family drive, my son Robert told his brothers a story he called "The Legend of Butt-Crack Man." Robert's story had the whole car "cracking" up for two hours straight.)

But being funny isn't always as easy as it looks. More than once I have tried a joke in my writing only to see it fall flat. So how do you do it? Is being funny something you're born with, like the ability to wiggle your ears? Is it one of those things that either you can do or you can't? No. Whether or not you're naturally funny in real life, you can learn to be funny on paper. Here are a few tips for incorporating humor into your writing:

Choose the right details for your story. A man hanging from a cliff by his fingernails—not funny. But a man hanging by one armpit hair—now that's funny!

Don't expect **silly names** to generate too much humor. Giving characters names like Mrs. Dillybobble or Darius Roofus Maddenfoofer only goes so far to make your story funny.

Use puns and word-play. At my sister's wedding six little flower girls collided in the church aisle and fell into a tangled heap. The church erupted in laughter, and my cousin muttered, "What a cute-astrophe!"

Think surprise. Make sure your writing isn't too predictable. Here's an example of giving readers something they don't expect:

Bring **humorous situations** from your life or imagination into your writing. Although we consider ourselves to be unique individuals, in fact we are much more alike than we are different. Chances are, if you think something is funny, your readers will, too.

I bought a foot-long hot dog and dressed it just the way I always do—mustard on one side of the dog, ketchup along the other side, and plenty of relish piled on top. By the time I was finished my mouth was watering. I carried the fully loaded hot dog to Cliff Proctor—and stuffed it down the back of his shirt.

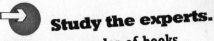

Study the experts.
Look for examples of books where the authors weave humor into their writing. One of my favorite funny passages is in Gary Paulsen's novel <u>Harris and Me</u> where Harris pees on the electric wire.

One note of caution: guy humor can get guys into trouble. (The North Face company was not amused by Winkelmann's clothing line. In fact, they filed a lawsuit against the South Butt. But believe it or not, this delighted Winkelmann because the lawsuit generated priceless publicity for his company.)

Guy humor can sound disrespectful to some teachers. Be smart about how you use it—and how extreme you go. In a school context, you may have to dial it back a bit. A teacher who reads something of yours and thinks you're being too much of a wise guy can make life difficult for you. If you calmly explain what you're trying to do, and use words such as *satire* or *parody*, the teacher might be more receptive to what you're writing.

Brandon, a seventh-grader in Washington State, decided to write a poem with sports as the theme. His class had been studying haiku poetry for several weeks when Brandon had a sudden flash of inspiration. Perhaps he could write a parody of the haiku and call it a "lowku." As Brandon envisioned it, such a poem would follow the same format as a haiku but could speak to the negative or less beautiful side of the theme. Here is Brandon's lowku poem:

> I walk in the room
> Off goes the sweaty jock strap
> I feel so relieved

Good writing sticks in your mind, and Brandon's lowku poem certainly does that. I admire the way he was able to take this ancient form of poetry and morph it to suit his purpose. This poem is fresh and original. And I LOVE the idea of the lowku (which reminds me of *Guyku*, a book of poetry by Bob Raczka). Hey, how many people can say that they invented a new form of poetry?

Riding the Vomit Comet

Writing About Disgusting Stuff

When I was growing up, there was a boy in our neighborhood we called Deak, a kid who was nice but also gullible beyond belief. To set the stage for this story, it's important to know that at this particular time our family pets were a dozen half-grown roosters. These crazy little critters spent their time wandering around our house, front yard and back, feasting on bugs and spiders. Unfortunately, they also pooped all over the place. We would step on the smelly stuff, get it on our shoes, and track it into the house, which sent my mother into shrieks of outrage.

One summer day, my brother Tommy scraped up a smear of chicken dung and presented it to Deak at the end of a stick.

"Have a bite," my brother said, flashing his friendliest smile. "It tastes like candy."

Deak had a bad cold that day. With his nose all stuffed up, he couldn't smell anything.

"Really?" Deak said.

"Uh-huh," my brother insisted. "It's tasty."

I stood watching this scene unfold, too stunned to move or speak. The stick—and what was on the end of it—glinted in the morning sunlight. If you didn't know better, you'd think it might have been a smear of brownie batter.

"Okay," Deak said, blinking those big, brown, I'll-believe-anything-you-tell-me eyes of his.

When he opened his mouth, my brother reached forward. A second later Deak's mouth closed around the end of the stick. His eyes closed, too.

Time stopped.

Suddenly his eyes flew open. He gagged, spit, and then raced home, howling like a mortally wounded animal.

Tommy had gotten in trouble countless times before (in fact just about every day of his life), but he sensed that this just might be the Grand Pooh-bah of All Troubles. There was nothing he could do to undo what he had just done. So Tommy did the only logical thing: he ran up to his bedroom and hid under the bed. There he cowered, trembling, awaiting the inevitable.

One minute later the phone rang.

It was Deak's mother. Telling Mom exactly what Tommy just did to her innocent son. Mom raced upstairs, pulled Tommy out from under the bed, and proceeded to paddle his sorry butt with a hairbrush.

Let's take a moment to unpack this story. There are a few things I want you to notice.

I didn't shy away from the subject matter. This story is written in a direct, straightforward way.

I balanced the **external** (what was *happening*) with the **internal** (how the characters were *feeling*).

I didn't rush the pacing of the story. There's a beginning, middle, and end. I took the time to describe the chicken poop, which "glinted in the morning light." Notice also that I included moments of silence in the story, such as the pause between the time when Deak tasted the stuff and when he suddenly realized what he had just put into his mouth.

Popular movies often create situations involving distasteful stuff: body fluids, garbage, and so on. Writers do, too. As readers we cringe, grit our teeth, but at the same time we can't turn away because such subjects really can be fascinating.

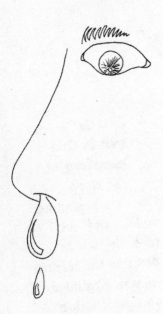

As a writer, it's fine to include revolting stuff in your writing, but just mentioning it isn't enough. You've got to make sure that the "movie" of your writing comes alive for the reader. You have to write it in such a way that your readers will picture exactly what's going on.

My novels include several disgusting descriptions. At the beginning of *Fig Pudding*, I describe a little brother with a cold: "two fat jets of greenish snot were slowly making their way down his face from nose to mouth."

In my young adult novel *The One O'Clock Chop*, Matt finds a dead body while digging clams. After the waterlogged body gets hauled onto the boat, Matt stares in horrified fascination.

BOOGERS

Boogers, boogers,
Nice and sticky,
They taste good,
With milk and cookies.

> I'd never seen a dead person before, and the
> drowned corpse looked pretty gruesome—the
> too-white skin, the man's tongue hanging out
> like a strip of wide soggy ribbon. There was a
> strand of seaweed on the chin. I stared at the
> mouth. The blue lips actually moved! Could this
> man possibly be alive? Trying to speak? Then I
> was horrified to see the lips part. An eel slithered
> out of the man's mouth, green, about eight
> inches long.

I had never actually seen a drowned person before, so I had to use my imagination. I drew upon what I had learned from books, newspapers, even TV and movies, about people who have drowned. I knew that I wanted to end with a particularly gross detail to show the main character's reaction; that's why I included the eel.

Describing a drowned man is serious business. But disgusting writing can also be wickedly funny. In this story from *Knucklehead*, by Jon Scieszka, bedlam erupts when six brothers plus one cat suddenly start vomiting during a car ride.

Car Trip

> Of all the Scieszka brother memories, I believe
> it was a family car trip that gave us our finest

moment of brotherhood. We were driving cross-country from Michigan to Florida, all of us, including the family cat (a guy cat, naturally), in the family station wagon. Somewhere mid-trip we stopped at one of those Stuckey's rest-stop restaurants to eat and load up on Stuckey's candy.

We ate lunch, ran around like maniacs in the warm sun, then packed back into the station wagon—Mom and Dad up front, Jim, Jon, Tom, Gregg, Brian, Jeff, and the cat in back. Somebody dropped his Stuckey's Pecan Log Roll on the floor. The cat found it and must have scarfed every bit of it, because two minutes later we heard that awful *ack ack ack* sound of a cat getting ready to barf.

The cat puked up the pecan nut log. Jeff, the youngest and smallest (and closest to the floor), was the first to go. He got one look and whiff of the pecan-nut cat yack and blew his own sticky lunch all over the cat. The puke-covered cat jumped on Brian. Brian barfed on Gregg. Gregg upchucked on Tom. Tom burped a bit of Stuckey lunch back on Gregg. Jim and I rolled down the windows and hung out as far as we could, yelling in group-puke horror.

Dad didn't know what had hit the back of the

car. No time to ask questions. He just pulled off to the side of the road. All of the brothers—Jim, Jon, Tom, Gregg, Brian, and Jeff—spilled out of the puke wagon and fell in the grass, gagging and yelling and laughing until we couldn't laugh anymore.

What does it all mean? What essential guy wisdom did I learn from this?

Stick with your brothers. Stick up for your brothers. And if you ever drop a pecan nut log in a car with your five brothers and the cat . . . you will probably stick *to* your brothers.

We have cats in our house, so I'm all too familiar with the *ack-ack-ack* sound of a cat getting ready to throw up. Notice the synonyms Scieszka used for vomiting—*barf, upchuck, yack, puke, blew his lunch*—to avoid using the same word over and over.

If you want to write about a revolting event or incident in a way that will bring it alive, here are a few more tips to keep in mind.

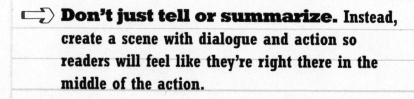

Don't just tell or summarize. Instead, create a scene with dialogue and action so readers will feel like they're right there in the middle of the action.

➡️ **Describe your characters.** In the first example, I let readers know how incredibly gullible Deak was. That sets the stage for him trusting my brother and eating the you-know-what.

➡️ **Use sensory details:** smell, touch, sound, taste, sight.

➡️ **Take your time.** Don't rush through it.

Oh, and one more thing. I didn't describe that dead body because I wanted to make my readers cringe but because it was an important event in the book. Whatever disgusting thing you describe shouldn't be included simply to gross out your readers. Rather, it should be a necessary part of the story or poem you're trying to create.

an interview
with

JON SCIESZKA

Jon Scieszka has written tons of popular books, including *The True Story of the 3 Little Pigs*, the Time Warp Trio series, and *Math Curse*. I recently read and loved *Knucklehead*, his zany autobiography. One reason I connected with that book is that he grew up as one of six brothers, just like me. Jon is keenly interested in boy readers and writers. He has a great Web site titled GuysRead.com. Check it out!

Ralph In Knucklehead you have a knack for finding words and expressions (knucklehead, rectum, "Stop breathing my air!" and "We broke Gregg") that are hilarious. Could you say something about your relationship with or attitude toward words in general?

JON

Knucklehead is one of those words that really is a keeper. It just sounds so good, and so right in describing a . . . knucklehead. I don't consciously keep a list or book of words. But when I hear a good one, I do tend to use it and use it until someone tells me to stop, or I write a story using it. In my book of Aesop-style fables, *Squids Will Be Squids,* I wrote the whole fable of "Horseshoe Crab vs. Blowfish" after I overheard two first-graders arguing on the playground, and the one guy called the other one a "spankinghead." Neither one of the kids (or me) knew what the heck it meant. But we all knew perfectly that it meant something not good.

Ralph Do you revise much?

JON Oh, yes. Word choice and sentence pacing is everything in writing humor. I rewrite all of my stories at least ten times, sometimes as many as twenty. I read the pieces aloud to an audience. And I can tell right away what needs to be taken out, what needs to be added in, what needs to be buried in my drawer and not taken out again. It's like practicing to tell a joke really well.

Ralph You didn't hesitate to tackle edgy topics in <u>Knucklehead</u> like cat vomit, peeing on heaters, and the like. What advice would you give to a boy who wants to include gross stuff in a story? I'm interested in both your thoughts about how to get away with it in a school setting as well as practical advice on the writer's craft.

JON Because I was the first National Ambassador for Young People's Literature, I can get away with writing about cat puke, dirt clod wars, and peeing on my little brothers. (I actually read the story about that last item to President and Mrs. Bush and a whole lot of people dressed up for the fancy ball when they gave me my ambassador medal in Washington, D.C.) I don't know if I could write the same stories if I was still in school. But if I was, here's what I would tell my writing teacher: "I thought I would work on including vivid, memorable sensory detail in my writing. That's why I have the cat making that awful 'ack-ack-ack' sound just before he barfs. And that is why, in the peeing on the heater story, I just had to use the awful smell of fried urine. Those details are memorable."

Believe it or not, I try to not cross the line of being gross just for the easy laugh. Those movies where somebody randomly gets kicked in the crotch or somebody randomly cuts a fart (or "passes gas" as my mom would say) are just not that funny to me. Those are lazy jokes. And lazy humor writing is the same—just not that funny to me.

Ralph
In Knucklehead you mentioned that you liked the violence in The Three Stooges. You threw dirt hand grenades while playing war. I did similar things as a kid. Many guys like to write (and read) about violent stuff. It seems like the world has changed so now boys are discouraged from violent play. Any thoughts on this?

JON
Kids have definitely lost some of that unsupervised playtime I had as a kid. And that unsupervised time is when a kid really grows up

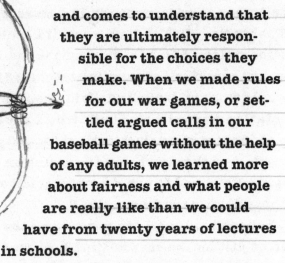

and comes to understand that they are ultimately responsible for the choices they make. When we made rules for our war games, or settled argued calls in our baseball games without the help of any adults, we learned more about fairness and what people are really like than we could have from twenty years of lectures in schools.

A lot of guys I know like to read and write violent stuff. And I think it's because guys are always testing themselves. They want to see what they can do. They want some action. They want something real. Some of my favorite books are books about the history of war. But I hardly ever see war books in school. If anyone should be reading books about war, it is our boys. They are the ones who end up having to fight the wars.

So why not read both <u>Pride and Prejudice</u> and <u>The Art of War</u>, <u>The Very Quiet Cricket</u> and also <u>Smash Crash</u>? I think boys become better readers when adults allow them to read the whole wide range of writing.

Ralph Your Trucktown books include lots of smashing and crashing. Did you deliberately decide to include conflict and violence to make the books more engaging to boys?

Jon

Smashing and crashing was exactly what my brothers and I did when we played with our trucks and cars when we were kids. So when I wrote Truck-town for the youngest readers, I consciously included that true kind of play that doesn't often make it into the preschool world. Much of nursery school and kindergarten is about sitting quietly. But having been a boy, I know that boys also need that time to be rough and active and a little bit wild.

Ralph The "Crossing Swords" chapter in <u>Knucklehead</u> really rang a bell. When my father threw half-smoked cigarettes in the toilet, my brothers and I eagerly crowded around the bowl to direct a withering aerial attack from above, hell-bent on destroying those nicotine warships.

Jon

Years after my brothers and I had all grown up (and become a little more toilet-trained), my mom told me that she seriously considered turning one whole bathroom wall into a baseball-stadium-style group urinal. That could have been either brilliant . . . or completely disgusting. Because we guys have the external equipment that makes creative urinating possible, we are called to complete our biological destiny. I had another story that didn't make it into

Knucklehead about being motivated to learn cursive writing so I could write my name in the snow without all of the painful stops-and-starts of printing. But I decided that was maybe just one too many urine-based stories.

Ralph You deal with many edgy topics (fire, injuries, swears) in your memoir. Do you have any thoughts about how a guy could write about such topics without going too far? How much is too much? How do you define that line?

I think the real art in writing about those **JON** topics that we know are going to freak some people out is to write in a way that avoids being too obvious or too gross. For example, when I wrote about accidentally sprinkling my younger brother Gregg in the bathroom, I never wrote something as direct as "we peed on Gregg." That is what happened, but it's much funnier in the story to have Gregg complain, "Mom! Jim and Jon peed on me!" It's dialogue. Not even from me. And then I can write about my mom correcting him. And it's even funnier.

The smallest word choice can make a great difference. In the paragraph above this one, in the second sentence, I could have written, "when I wrote the story about pissing on Gregg . . ." But I think "when I wrote about accidentally sprinkling . . ." is funnier because it takes the reader that extra second

or two to figure out what exactly I'm talking about.
The Reader Brain goes, "A lawn sprinkler? A watering
can? No! I get it! He just wrote about peeing on his
brother!" And because your readers work harder to
get the joke, they feel more rewarded.

Ralph Do you keep a writer's notebook or journal to
collect stuff for use in your writing? If so, I'd
love to hear how you use it, and what sorts of things
you collect.

Jon I collect all kinds of things that inspire my
writing—songs, pictures, newspaper articles, found
pieces of paper, sketches, diagrams, rocks, words,
dreams. I also keep a bunch of different notebooks
with random ideas and scribbles and snatches of
dialogue or story ideas that come to me when I'm
reading or watching a movie, or sitting and thinking.
Then, when I get a story going that I like, I start
keeping all of the notes for that idea in its own
notebook. And I have a giant corkboard that covers
one whole wall of my studio, just to the side of my
desk, that I layer with stuff that I think about
including in my book. The latest thing I've been
working on is a middle-grade reader series about three
not-very-bright aliens who invade Earth. They
invade it by disguising themselves as fifth-graders.
They are Spaceheadz. That is the name of the
series—Spaceheadz. So right now my board is covered

with pictures of whales, ant nests, and radiation waves, diagrams of solar systems, lists of advertising slogans, codes, crop circles, kids' artwork, street art, and graffiti.

Ralph   Many guy writers end up in classrooms where the teacher gives a cold shoulder to the topics boys want to write about. Do you have any advice for boy writers who want to develop their craft?

JON

I would recommend that boy writers first have a discussion with their teacher about exactly the kind of things they would like to be both reading and writing. I know a lot of teachers, and I think every one of them would be thrilled to hear from their boys. It's about choice, about negotiating what is acceptable for school. Of course you won't be able to write some of the lyrics to your favorite songs, but you should be able to make a case for being able to read and write about war, wrestling, extreme fighting, and maybe even writing your name in the snow in cursive.

Boys should also feel free to invoke the name of the Ambassador and suggest that their teacher check in with Jon Scieszka. I would be glad to step up and give my official recommendation for guys to read and write what really interests them.

Writes of Blood, Battles, and Gore

uys love to write about battles and war. Some adults have trouble understanding that guys don't do this for some sinister purpose—we do it for fun! My sons filled countless notebooks with stories involving fierce battles, traps, ambushes, fiery explosions, attack and counter-attack. Sometimes they re-created stories they had seen in the movies or in video games: *Warcraft*, *Star Wars*, even *Teenage Mutant Ninja Turtles*. At other times they would borrow the characters they'd seen on TV or the movies and create their own versions and spin-offs.

But they had just as much fun inventing their own characters and concocting new stories with wild plots. When Joseph and his friend Jarod were in fourth grade, they created a wonderful set of stories called the Mushroom Wars. This series started through drawing. Many mushrooms have a little cap on top, which looks like a war helmet. Once they realized they could draw helmeted mushroom warriors—BINGO!—they were off and running.

When my son Robert and his friend Connor were about the same age they invented a series called the Fighting Fruit. These boys had a blast coming up with inventive names for the characters, including

Amputating Apple
Angry Orange
Battling Banana
Cherry Bomb
Exploding Apricot
Extreme Strawberry
Japanese Ginger
Pear of Aces
Stunned Starfruit
Torturing Tomato
Wicked Watermelon

Robert and Connor ended up writing a whole series with thrilling battles and adventures: "The Fighting Fruits' Archenemy," "The Fighting Fruits' Vacation," and "The Fighting Gummies."

WEAPONS

Robert went through a phase when he was obsessed with swords. He found several internet sites that sold all varieties of sword replicas, and would spend hours studying them. My wife was a little concerned about this, but I assured her that most guys go through a period when they're fascinated by guns and swords. One thing that makes weapons intriguing is that they come in so many varieties: clubs, blowguns, slingshots, lances, spears, morning stars, crossbows, hunting knives, BB guns, bazookas, flamethrowers, Molotov cocktails, just to name a few.

Weapons give you another way to develop your character. Consider Robin Hood or the elf Legolas in Tolkien's *Lord of the Rings*. These men always carried their bows and were deadly marksmen. Their weapons were extensions of their personalities: silent, stealthy, and dangerous.

Randall and Jared, eleven-year-old twins, invented a character named Chainsaw Bob. They created an adventure series for him. The word *chainsaw* makes me think of those gruesome Texas Chainsaw Massacre movies, but Chainsaw Bob never killed or maimed anybody. In fact, he wasn't a force of destruction. He simply carried around a chainsaw at all times, something that made him seem both odd and menacing. The chainsaw gave him a reserved source of power, making him more dangerous, even if he never used it against people.

There is one weapon described in chilling detail at the very beginning of *The Graveyard Book* by Neil Gaiman.

There was a hand in the darkness, and it held a knife.

The knife had a handle of polished black bone, and a blade finer and sharper than any razor. If it sliced you, you might not even know you had been cut, not immediately.

The knife had done almost everything it was

brought to that house to do, and both the blade
and the handle were wet.

This lead grabs the reader by the throat and won't let
go. The knife seems to be its own living character, even
more so than the man who carries it through the house.

BLOOD

There are two kinds of blood in the stories that guys like
to write: real blood and what I'll call *atmospheric* or *back-ground* blood. Let's start with the second one first. Sometimes in a story you want to include blood to create a
certain kind of mood or feeling. When my son Robert
was eleven years old, he received money for Christmas
and begged me to take him to a video game store. The
first video game he wanted to buy was labeled T (teenager). The second was M (mature).

"You're not a teenager yet," I told him. "You're too
young for those games."

Robert rolled his eyes. "Dad, I've played them before!"

"Sorry. We're not buying them."

"I'll turn off the blood," Robert offered.

Well, that shut me up. Until that moment I never knew
that there was an option to "turn off the blood" in order
to make video games less gory. When Robert promised to

turn off the blood, I reluctantly agreed to let him buy the game.

If you are writing a story where you can turn the blood on or off, you're probably using blood to create a certain kind of feeling or atmosphere. Let's say you're describing a bedroom in an old house: "Blood came surging up from the floorboards, flooding into the room through the heating vents. . . ." This certainly makes a vivid image, but you don't get the sense that it's actual blood from real people. It's fake, like the red stuff they use while filming a horror movie.

Take a look at this piece by Zack Smith, a fifth-grader in Maine:

> He comes into the room swinging all black, but the inside of his cape is red. Even his short hair is black. He opens his mouth and shows white fangs, and deep red blood drips down his chin. He hisses like an anaconda. He moves stealthily in the shadows. Then all of a sudden he is gone, and you feel something furry brush by your face: the flap of wings. Then it goes into a slim beam of light shining through the window made by the moon. You realize it's a bat. It flies right near you and you see it's not an ordinary bat; it's him.
>
> Right before your eyes he changes into his

normal form. When he is really close you can
see how pale he is. His skin is as white as snow.
As he walks toward you, your muscles tense.
The floorboards creak. Right behind you on a
table you feel for a flashlight. You turn around
quickly and grab it, but before you can turn it
on he swats it out of your hands. It hits the floor
with a crash. The light breaks. He gets right up
in your face—you can smell his cold stale old
breath. He slides his finger down your face. As
soon as his finger touches your face, icy cold
feeling shoots into your body. He hisses again
and then as quick as a viper he snaps. Your
whole world goes black. The last sound you hear
is his evil ear-piercing laughter.

The trick to creating a strong piece of writing like this
is to make it seem believable even when you and your
reader both know it's not. Zack does a great job of building tension by allowing the scene to unfold slowly, with
precise details (a slim beam of light). The "deep red blood"
that drips down his chin is only one part of the larger
scene.

Vampire blood is make-believe, but real blood is a whole
different thing. While sledding one day, my little brother
slid off an icy trail and into a branch, cutting his ear so
badly the earlobe was hanging by a tiny patch of skin. It

was hard to believe so much blood (so bright against the white snow) could come from an itty-bitty earlobe!

Bloody wounds and actual death are no joking matter. If you are writing about killing a deer on a hunting trip with your father, for instance, you want to be descriptive and even vivid, but you probably don't want to glorify the bloodshed, or describe it in a way that suggests you're taking delight in it. Rather, you want to show respect for the dead animal. Here are tips for using blood effectively in your writing:

Write it straight-ahead. **Don't shy away from the blood.** Describe it the way you would describe anything else, using your five senses.

Use slow motion. Bloodshed is usually the result of some accident or violent incident. Don't rush through this part of the story. Write it in slow motion, using frame-by-frame action to show the reader exactly how the bloody event happened. You might even give some of the internal dialogue (what the character is saying to him- or herself) when it happened.

Select **vivid details** that give readers a picture of what's going on. Here is an excerpt from a story written by a boy named Ryan. Look at this description of what happened when Ryan's brother took a nasty fall and gashed his leg on a piece of jagged iron:

My older cousin Mike worked hard to stop the bleeding. I fetched a bag of clean rags and they pressed them against the wound, but at first it didn't work. I kept getting more and more rags. Those rags were white when I handed them to him, but they were bright red when he gave them back to me.

That detail about the rags in the final sentence creates a powerful image readers won't easily forget.

Study the experts. Take a close look at the Redwall series by Brian Jacques. The struggle between Martin and Tsarmina toward the end of *Mossflower* is an excellent example of a fight-to-the-death battle scene. In the Suggested Reading section I've put together a list of other "bloody books" in which you can see skillful writing in this area.

Don't overdo blood and guts. While visiting a middle school in Colorado, I went to a sixth-grade language arts class that was being taught by Mr. Cole. He smiled at me when I walked into the room.

"Let's ask Mr. Fletcher what he thinks."

One of the kids raised his hand; I nodded at him.

"What do you think about gore?" he asked.

Well, I had never been asked THAT question. For a moment I just stood there, feeling the eyes of the class upon me, trying to figure out a suitable reply.

"Gore?" I smiled and shrugged. "I think he could have been a pretty good president."

I guess it was a lame joke because the kids just stared at me. Only Mr. Cole managed a laugh. I cleared my throat and tried again.

"When it comes to blood and gore," I said, "a little goes a long way. Don't overdo it. Take for instance 'The Tell-Tale Heart' by Edgar Allan Poe, one of the most famous short stories ever published. True, there's a murder in that story. But there are no arteries cut, no blood spurting out. Sure, it's intense, but it's not in-your-face and graphic."

Try not to exaggerate when you incorporate bloody material. Notice how Gaiman described the knife in the excerpt I cited earlier. He could have said that the knife was *dripping with blood*. Instead he merely said it was *wet*. He's leaving room for readers to figure it out for themselves, to say, "Aha, I know why that knife is wet!" As a writer, it's important to know when to push the edge, but it's just as important to know when to pull back.

Here's a poem by Austin, a fourth-grader. I like the way he takes a familiar subject and makes it come alive by describing a fierce battle between the sun and the night.

Morning

The sun
appears
on the horizon.
A knight in
flaming armor.
He comes
for vengeance:
a battle
against night.
The sound
of metal
hitting
metal.
Then
the day
begins.

When you think about it, strong writing is not about bloodshed but about bravery, survival, the will to live, and so forth. Those are some of the themes you want to leave in your readers' minds when they've finished what you have written.

Superheroes and Fantasy

My published novels are all realistic fiction. This strikes me as funny considering what my four sons prefer to read: fantasy. They have devoured countless books by Rick Riordan, J. R. R. Tolkien, Brian Jacques, Neil Gaiman, Cornelia Funke, Orson Scott Card, Nancy Farmer, and of course, J. K. Rowling. And they are not alone. Millions of boys, as well as girls, have been drawn to the world of fantasy, with its intense battles, larger-than-life characters, and mind-boggling plot twists. Fantasy may be compelling to read, but writing it is harder than it looks. For one thing, in the world of fantasy everything gets super-sized. We encounter larger-than-life characters and immense plots that unfold in vast new worlds. Not only that, but in this genre just about anything goes: a character can grow three heads, morph into the body of an eagle, then travel forward two centuries in time. The endless possibilities can be overwhelming.

This is a HUGE subject—entire books have been written on how to write fantasy—so I'm not going to go into great depth here. But I will share a few tips for how to improve your writing in this genre. I hope you'll try these suggestions, but at the same time, don't expect instant magic. These tips won't work every time. The more you play with them, the more comfortable and skillful you'll get at putting them to work.

Let's start with the bones, the skeleton of the story. Like any fiction, fantasy writing contains three basic elements: characters, setting, and plot. Let's take a brief look at how you can develop each of these elements. Note: Although fantasy does not always contain a superhero, for the purposes of this book I have combined these two kinds of writing in this discussion.

SUPERHEROES

The most famous superheroes were "born" either in comic books (Batman, Flash, Punisher, Spider-Man) or in cartoons (Freakazoid, ThunderCats). Later they would star in movies. Many popular superheroes originated in the world of mythology. Greek gods and heroes set the stage for the comic book heroes of the 1930s and 1940s. Hercules, for example, is clearly the precursor to the Hulk.

Of course, when you write, there's no reason to limit yourself to the superheroes that have already been created; you can design your own. Here are a couple of examples of superheroes created by boys:

Beans, Hamster and Secret Agent.
This character was created by Zander, a kid who based the story on his own pet hamster. Zander wrote an exciting series about Beans whose titles include <u>Beans the Hero</u>, <u>Beans Returns</u>, and <u>Beans Back in Action</u>.

Snorlax. My sons Robert and Joseph created this character: a big, soft, hairy creature who slept most of the time and ate nothing but Twinkies.

Once you've got your superhero or main character in the fantasy you're writing, there's a new challenge: how do you bring that character alive for the reader? You should be able to clearly picture the character in your mind—clothes, weapons, and scars—so you can describe him or her in your writing. You should know the big things (his supernatural powers) as well as the little stuff (favorite foods, peculiar habits). You should know your character well enough to name exactly what items he or she would pack for a journey.

Writing Tip: *In addition to describing the superhero's fabulous strengths and powers, don't forget to include that character's weaknesses. Every superhero has a frailty, human element, or limitation. Yes, Superman can fly, but he is vulnerable to red and green kryptonite. A bullet to the head could kill Batman. The Incredible Hulk may be powerful, but he's not very smart.*

It's very important to explain your superhero's weakness. Doing so will accomplish several things. For one, it makes your character more complex and believable. Readers can relate to someone who isn't perfect, who has faults and weaknesses like any mortal being. But in addition, that weakness can create intriguing possibilities for plot tension. Let's say, for instance, that your superhero is invincible in water. What then happens when he pursues the villain to the Sahara?

ViLLAiNS

In a strong piece of fantasy, the villain is as important as the superhero. Your villain should be realistic and human enough for readers to identify with. One way to do that is to give the villain some redeeming qualities. Mix in a smidgen of good along with all that evil. Gollum (Lord of the Rings) is scheming and deceitful, sure enough, but knowing his history—how he happened to find the Ring and how it corrupted him—makes us feel sympathy toward him. Gollum suddenly becomes a far more interesting character.

Writing Tip: *Although we try to endow superheroes with omnipotent strength and power, in fact the bad guys must be every bit as smart and powerful as the good guys. Otherwise, the superhero will quickly crush his or her opponent and the story will end as fast as it began. What fun is that?*

Jane Yolen is not a guy writer, but she has been writing first-rate fantasy for thirty-five years. She knows this genre inside and out.

"I give my villains a backstory (much of which never gets onto the page!), and I give them their own reasons for doing what they do," Jane told me. "No villain ever really considers himself or herself purely bad. They just don't count the suffering of others as any account."

Jane also told me that when she writes fantasy and creates characters, she often thinks of the people in her life and uses them as models.

"I usually pattern them after one or several friends or family," she says. "In my book *Dragon's Blood,* Jakkin is my son Adam, smart, courageous, and often clueless. Akki is patterned after my daughter Heidi—smart, smart-mouthed, willing to step out of line if it's the right thing to do, heedless of her own danger."

SETTiNG

Think of Hogwarts School of Witchcraft and Wizardry, or Middle Earth in Lord of the Rings. In a strong piece of writing, the setting almost becomes another character in the story, with its own "personality" that captures the imagination of the reader. When writing fantasy, it is especially important to know the world where your story takes place. You should be able to see it in your mind: mountains, caves, landscape features, wormholes to another world, the bizarre-looking creatures that inhabit it.

How do this world and its creatures differ from what is found on planet Earth?

Make sure you devote a few sentences (or more) to describing the world where the action takes place. The setting of your fantasy should do at least two things: it should set the tone for your story, and it should have an impact on the plot. In the first page of *The Hobbit,* Tolkien describes a hobbit home, a place that is safe, dry, and comfortable. Bilbo will have to leave this cozy world when he ventures forth to fight Smaug, the dragon.

By contrast, let's take a close look at the first paragraph of "The Long Rain," a short story by Ray Bradbury. This story takes place on the planet Venus, where it rains constantly.

> The rain continued. It was a hard rain, a perpetual rain, a sweating and steaming rain; it was a mizzle, a downpour, a fountain, a whipping at the eyes, an undertow at the ankles; it was a rain to drown all rains and the memory of rains. It came by the pound and the ton, it hacked at the jungle and cut the trees like scissors and shaved the grass and tunneled the soil and molted the bushes. It shrank men's hands into the hands of wrinkled apes; it rained a solid glassy rain, and it never stopped.

In the world Bradbury creates, the never-ending rain becomes an ominous force that not only makes the main characters miserable; it threatens their very survival.

PLOT

Good guys battle the bad guys. You create an engaging plot using all your writing skills and everything you know about what makes good writing: strong lead, dialogue, suspense, details that will stick in the reader's mind, and a satisfying conclusion.

Young writers often create fantasy that is a series of episodes and adventures: first we teleported to planet Xexa to zap some bad guys, next we got beamed to Catastrophia where we battled the deadly brain-eating Deformers, and after that . . . While this kind of story can be fun to write, it doesn't add up to much and might lead your reader to wonder impatiently, Okay, but what's the point?

Strong fantasy should include a larger, all-encompassing conflict. Ideally, you should be able to explain the plot in one sentence. Lord of the Rings contains many battles and subplots, but the main plot involves Frodo's journey to Mordor, his quest to throw the Ring into the fiery Cracks of Doom. In *The Wizard of Oz*, Dorothy wants to bring the witch's broomstick to the Wizard so she can return to her family in Kansas.

The plots in this genre often involve the main character

facing hardships, undergoing a difficult journey, or making a quest. These journeys are usually internal as well as physical. Yes, Luke Skywalker battles the Empire, but at the same time he is trying to come to grips with the legacy of his father. As the main character undertakes the journey or quest, we should also see him gain wisdom and maturity. Thus, when you create your plot, think not only about *what* experiences the character will undergo, but also *why*.

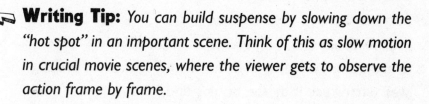

Writing Tip: *You can build suspense by slowing down the "hot spot" in an important scene. Think of this as slow motion in crucial movie scenes, where the viewer gets to observe the action frame by frame.*

MAGIC

Spells, charms, voodoo, hexes, potions, and invisible shields are tremendous fun. But before you introduce magic to your story, think it through. What impact does the magic have on the world? How does it change the balance of power between the hero and villains? How will regular people react to the magic?

And once you create the rules of the world, you have to stick to those rules and be consistent. The world of Harry Potter contains all sorts of delightful magical touches, but there are definite limits, too. You would never see the

Dementors showing up armed with machine guns or hand grenades. Such a scene could never happen in the world Rowling creates. As you write your story, you should continually ask yourself, Does this make sense in the fantasy world of my story?

I would caution against getting too caught up in magical gizmos and gadgets. The magic should serve the story, not the other way around. But if you do mention a magical thingamajig near the beginning of your story, the reader will expect you to do something with it, so be sure to carry it through in some way.

Jane Yolen says, "If you make a big deal of a wand or a dragon or an opening door for time travel, well, you darn well better use it by the book's end."

Writing Tip: *In a fantasy story, a person must have limits to his/her magical abilities. Otherwise, the story has no conflict: the magic can quickly overwhelm the other side.*

Fantasy can contain all varieties of magic, including time travel. But those aren't the most important things to remember when writing fantasy. Think about *The Wizard of Oz*, or *The Lion, the Witch, and the Wardrobe*. Ultimately, your challenge is to create an engaging story about another world, one that will linger in the mind of the reader after the final word.

GREG TRINE

Greg Trine is the author of the uproarious Melvin Beederman, Superhero series. The titles of these books give a good idea of what readers can expect: *The Curse of the Bologna Sandwich*, *Terror in Tights*, and *The Brotherhood of the Traveling Underpants*. Greg lives with his family in California. He loves chocolate and likes to spend time inventing new flavors of ice cream. His latest is Rainbow Trout Ripple.

Ralph Can you talk about your writing process? Do you plan out your story ahead of time (outline or storyboard), or do you feel your way along as you write?

GREG I generally don't outline before I start writing. For me, what makes a book worth reading is the writing . . . and no amount of prewriting or outlining will tell you whether or not you can make the paragraphs work. What usually guides me is knowledge of what a story is. A character faces a problem, and things are going to get worse before they get better. Before I start writing, though, I do have to know my ending.

Ralph I've heard that you never read comics when you were a kid, so you have no preconceived notions of how a superhero should act. How do you create a superhero?

GREG I think I probably got lucky with Melvin. He's a very unique character, and I'm happy to have stumbled across him. I think he's more interesting because he's so flawed . . . flying problems, train-stopping problems, X-ray vision problems. I would recommend including both strengths and weaknesses in your superhero. One of my favorite superheroes is Spider-Man, a classic example of a flawed hero. You gotta feel for a guy who can bench-press a bus but can't talk to the girl.

Ralph It seems that having a compelling bad guy (like the Joker in Batman) can really lift the quality of the story. Your books contain all kinds of humorous bad guys like the McNasty brothers and the Spaz brothers. Do you do anything in particular to make your bad guys interesting?

GREG Since my books are for a fairly young age, I feel I can be as goofy as I want to be. Basically, what I look for in a villain is humor, and that usually begins with a funny name. If I have more than one bad guy in a story, I look for ways to set them apart from each other . . . in the way they talk, for instance. I think about which one is in charge, and does being in charge cause some interesting conflict between them.

Ralph Could you share any thoughts about how to incorporate humor in writing?

GREG I guess there's a reason it's called a "sense" of humor. A writer should pay attention to what he/she thinks is funny. Write to make yourself laugh, and don't get too caught up in what you think your reader will think is funny. I usually just let myself go and find the humor along the way.

Also, I generally avoid potty humor. The reason is what I mentioned above . . . it doesn't make me laugh, and I feel I need to pay attention to that. When all else fails, write for yourself. You'll draw from a deeper well and will have a better chance of connecting with your readers and making them laugh.

Ralph The books in the Melvin Beederman series are flat-out zany. You give yourself permission to let the story go in any direction—even having a character escape from one book and break into the narrator's house! How do you keep your stories fresh and inventive? Or, to put it another way, how do you resist getting formulaic and predictable?

GREG

Some of the wackiness in my books happened spontaneously as I was writing. The real test was when my editor was okay with it. It gave me the confidence to push it a little further in each book.

Again, these books are for a fairly young audience. I probably wouldn't have been able to pull it off and make it believable if I was writing for an older age. Being fresh and inventive is a tough one when writing a series. I try to vary the villains as much as possible with each book. Sometimes they work alone . . . sometimes they're in pairs . . . and I have at least one trio of bad guys.

Ralph Even though your stories are pretty wacky, there does seem to be a method to your madness. Can you say something about internal consistency or plausibility in writing fantasy?

GREG

Yes, even though the stories are outlandish, they aren't overly so, and this comes back to paying attention to your own sense of humor and your sense of story. The Melvin stories actually make sense within the world that I created for him. A colleague of mine wrote a story where the main character's stomach talks to him. I told him that it was too absurd to be funny. Going over the top just to go over the top rarely works. I keep reminding myself what a story is—a character with a problem that gets worse before it gets better—and that helps me make it plausible.

Ralph What other writers do you admire?

Probably too many to mention, but here goes: **GREG**
Sid Fleischman, Rodman Philbrick, Jerry
Spinelli, Graham McNamee, Walter Dean Myers,
John Green, and many more. For some reason,
I really connect with other male writers. Guy
stuff—yes!

Sports Writing

Sports writing is a big umbrella that includes many subcategories: sports fiction, nonfiction and biography, reporting, commentary, and how-to. These are all worthy genres, but in this chapter I will focus mostly on the stories involving sports (fiction, realistic stories, memoir) that boys like to write. I have lots to say on this subject, but the most important thing is (drumroll, please) . . .

DEVELOP YOUR CHARACTERS

Consider this story I started to write:

> Austin stepped up to the plate and cocked his bat. After a brief pause, the pitcher rocked back and fired the first pitch, a fastball on the outside corner. Strike one! Austin thought it was a ball, but didn't say anything to the ump. He got ready for the next pitch. Strike two!

Although a story like this throws the reader right into the action, it doesn't tell the reader much about Austin—who he is, what he's like, what's going on in his head. With good sports writing, you get a strong sense of who the characters are: their quirks,

fears, struggles, and obsessions. Here's another way I might write this piece:

Austin used his right hand to swing his bat in a wide circle once, twice, three times. Then he flipped the bat around and wrote the words *Say Hey* in the dirt. That was the nickname for his all-time favorite player. Willie Mays: the Say Hey Kid. Then, taking extreme care not to step on the white line, Austin stepped into the batter's box. He tapped the plate exactly seven times—not six, not eight—then pulled back the bat to await the pitch.

The catcher watched all this and laughed sarcastically, but Austin ignored him. He performed the same rituals every time he batted. They helped him to focus. Sure, he was superstitious, but what of it? Lots of pro ballplayers were superstitious, too. Outfielder Larry Walker was obsessed with the number three. Wade Boggs took exactly 150 ground balls during infield practice. Boggs took batting practice at exactly 5:17 p.m. every day and always ran wind sprints at 7:17.

In this second version, we get to know the superstitious side of Austin, which makes him more interesting. If readers care more about the characters in a story, they will care more about the action.

Think hard about the main characters in your story, not just as players in the game but also as people. Does he have a sore ankle he's trying to hide from the coach? Is he dreaming about a girl he's got a crush on? Is he worried about his little brother, who has been left home with no one else in the house? Showing other aspects of these people will help them come alive as three-dimensional characters.

One way of bringing a character to life is to show him talking to himself during crucial moments of the action.

This is called internal dialogue, something we all do. Let's say you're writing about a crucial at-bat in the ninth inning. You step into the batter's box.

> The first pitch was an inside curve ball I had to jacknife away from. Ball one. The second pitch was also a curve, which swerved outside. A 2–0 count. Take a breath, I told myself. Stay calm. He doesn't want to walk me, so there's no way he's going to try another curve. That would be way too risky. He's going to come in with a fastball. And I'll be ready for it.

ZERO IN ON THE IMPORTANT PARTS
Here's a story written by a fourth-grade kid:

> We were playing the South Field Beavers. In the first inning they only got one hit, no runs. In the bottom of the first I was batting fifth, but our team made three quick outs so I didn't get to bat. In the second inning Tommy, our center-fielder, made a nice running catch. They didn't score any runs. In the bottom of the second David Jocelyn struck out. I stepped into the batter's box. The pitcher threw it right down the middle. Strike one! I was more ready for the second pitch and smacked it into right field, our first hit.

This story continues for three pages. The narrator describes every inning. Since he had played in the game, this story was intensely interesting to him. He actually went through this experience and cared about who won the game. It must have been fun for him to relive that particular game by writing about it. However, most people who will read this story were not there and won't find this kind of story very interesting. Here are three tips for avoiding this kind of writing:

Summarize. This is crucial. Let's say you're writing about a baseball game, a pitchers' duel where the score was 1–1 in the seventh inning. Instead of telling what happened batter by batter, inning by inning, you could summarize it like this:

Both pitchers were firing bullets that day. Our pitcher had struck out eight batters. The other pitcher had nine strikeouts. By the seventh inning each team had managed only a single run.

This paragraph does two things: it gives a **quick recap** of the action, and it sets up a dramatic scene to follow.

Cut out the boring parts. In order to do this, you have to reread what you have written. Put brackets around any sections where you have described a play or action that didn't have a major impact on the final outcome. Now go back and reread the bracketed parts a second time. Would your story be better if you removed those parts? If so, show no mercy. Give 'em the ax!

Focus on the most important part. In a story, you should probably pick out one or two parts of the game. Choose carefully which parts you want to describe. Was that shot, catch, hit, or injury crucial to deciding the outcome of the game? Was it especially exciting? If so, describe it. You might even use **"slow motion"** (as I mentioned in chapter 4) to give the reader a freeze-frame, blow-by-blow description of what happened.

CRAFT A LiVELY LEAD TO HOOK THE READER

Rick Bragg once wrote an article about the Olympic sport luge. His article begins

> Picture riding the lid of a turkey roaster pan down a roller coaster rail after an ice storm.

> Picture it at almost 80 miles an hour, with
> wicked turns, at G-forces so powerful that you
> cannot raise your helmet from the ice, which
> glitters just an inch away.
>   Now picture making that ride face first.

What a lead! Honestly, I have never been very interested in the luge, but these three sentences grab my imagination and make it impossible to put this article down.

DESCRiBE THE SETTiNG

Depicting where the action takes place—the pool, tennis court, or soccer field—will help the reader picture what's going on. Look at all the sensory details Max Friedman (a fourth-grader) includes in his story about going to a New England Patriots game with his father:

> Thirty thousand fans welcomed me to Gillette
> Stadium. The players seemed to be waiting for
> me, with my blue Patriots jersey hanging over
> my shoulders. The ceiling creaked with the
> weight of the fans. The filthy floor was littered
> with gum and peanut shells. The vendors, who
> were wearing bright, yellow, corny polo shirts
> with the name of their restaurant sewed on the
> front, waved people in.

At the gift shop I chose a winter hat with the Patriots logo on the front. Red, white, and blue dreadlocks came down from every direction. I screwed it onto my head. At the food stand I bought a pulled pork sandwich that was the size of the moon. Strings of pulled pork bulged out of the bun, the meat drenched with BBQ sauce. My dad bought a container of popcorn, and then we headed back to our seats.

The Patriots' young defense was no match for the Ravens' dominant offense. Baltimore pulled ahead with a field goal and led 3–0.

A lot of the game was a blur. Fans screamed. Down on the field, players bellowed out orders. Water, soda, plastic bottles, peanut shells, and popcorn all swirled around in a rush of blustery wind. Bright lights flashed. Sweat stung my eyes. I tried to conquer the pulled pork sandwich and failed. It was just sooooo big. I was too full to eat dessert (doesn't happen too often). My colorful Rasta hat flapped around in the wind.

The quirky details in Max's story make it easy for me to identify with him as a narrator. The way he writes it, I feel like I am with him at Gillette Stadium.

DON'T OVERDO STATISTICS

Stats play a huge part in the world of sports, which is why guys love them. (As a kid, I could easily recite the batting averages, home run totals, and RBIs for all my favorite baseball players.) It's great to include this kind of data, but be careful not to overdo it. Weave them in where appropriate to enrich your story, but don't bury the reader in facts and stats.

GO BEYOND THE ACTION

Sports are crammed with action: vicious crosscheck, interception, leaping catch, last-minute goal. But a good writer also pays attention to the silences between the action. That's when you and your characters are thinking, reacting to what just happened, preparing for what will happen next. Those silences are also a good time to build suspense.

AVOID CLICHÉS!

A cliché is a group of words that has been used so many times it has become stale and has lost its effectiveness. Clichés are to be avoided in all writing, but for some reason they tend to sprout up in sports writing. For example,

Take it to the next level.
We gave it 110 percent.

This was a must-win ballgame.

Take it one game at a time.

They really came to play.

They just wanted it more.

We left it on the field.

He is their go-to guy.

He was a real thorn in our side.

We have to take care of business.

No need to throw him under the bus.

It goes with the territory.

They showed a lot of heart.

Our backs were against the wall.

He's swinging a hot bat.

Turn it up a notch.

Nothing but net.

The crowd was going wild.

We have to bring our A game.

A win is a win.

Try to be aware of clichés when you write and avoid them like the plague—er—well, you know what I mean!

SEEK OUT STRONG SPORTS WRITING

Great sports writing can be found in all kinds of places: newspapers, magazines, biographies, and novels. Read widely and don't be afraid to form your own opinion. Ask yourself, Is the writing strong and vivid, or is it weak and boring? Look at these two sentences from "Angus Bethune," a short story by Chris Crutcher.

> I am *incredibly* quick for a fat kid, and I have world-class reflexes. It is nearly impossible for the defensive lineman across from me to shake me, such are my anticipatory skills, and when I'm on defense I need only to lock in on a running back's hips to zero in on the tackle.

In these two sentences we learn a great deal about Angus as a football player. Even more important, we get to hear him talking. His voice—the way he says it—really comes alive and helps us to visualize him as a living, breathing character.

an interview
with

ROBERT LIPSYTE

Robert Lipsyte worked as a sports reporter for the *New York Times*. He has written some terrific books, including *The Contender*, *Center Field*, and *Raiders Night*. I asked him a few questions about the art and craft of writing sports novels.

Ralph When you write a sports novel, are you thinking first about the sport or about the characters? (Or both?)

ROBERT First off, I don't really think of them as sports novels, rather as stories with sports as a background. I've covered more sports than anything else (cops and city politics a distant second and third), so it means I don't need to do much research. Also, boys identify with sports easily and the kinds of problems [athletes] might face, and are more easily captured in the ethics and relationships around sports. But yes, I think of a character in some kind of conflict first, and then build the sports and the plot around it.

Ralph When boys write about sports, they often retell every play in the story. Their stories tend to be plot-heavy. Do you have any suggestions for avoiding that trap?

Winning or losing the game—usually as an indicator of your goodness or badness or need to learn some kind of a lesson—is the trap. And it's a hard one to avoid, especially when you're starting out. But even if you can't avoid the final score, you do need to lighten up on the game detail. It can get boring. One way is to tell the game through the emotions of the character and how he feels physically.

ROBERT

Ralph Do you keep a notebook to store ideas or tidbits you might use in future works?

I'd rather leave the house naked than without a pen and my little notebook. I'm always jotting things down. And once you start doing it, you observe more things, eavesdrop, and have more thoughts.

ROBERT

Ralph Are you thinking of place/setting when you write?

Sure. I close my eyes and try to imagine what it all looks like. But as with game detail, I try not to overdescribe. For instance, I try not to describe precisely what characters look like. It's important to let the reader do some work.

ROBERT

Ralph How much planning out or mapping do you do?

I have a skeleton outline—beginning, middle, and end—but over the years it's been getting less and less detailed because I change it so much. I find that as I write I get to know the characters better and the story reveals itself because I understand what the characters would do in each situation. But I still wouldn't start out without some kind of road map, even if I know I'll change directions.

Ralph Do you have any other advice or practical tips for guys who want to improve their writing in this area?

The basics:

- **READ other writers.**
- **REWRITE, REWRITE.**
- **POLISH.**

Beyond that, I think writers have to think of themselves as athletes playing word games. They have to be ready to show the same dedication, work ethic, willingness to refine technique and listen to constructive criticism as do successful athletes. Writing is hard work. You shouldn't do it unless you love doing it.

Freaky Stories

A few years ago friends and I rented a house in a remote part of Maine. We got off the ferry and found a taxi driver willing to drive us to the house where we were going to stay. After stowing our luggage in the trunk of the taxi, we climbed in and gave the driver our address.

"Two-twenty-one Oceanview Terrace."

For a while we just sat and enjoyed the views of rolling dunes and sparkling ocean. The driver kept quiet. I noticed that the guy was pretty jacked, with a thick mat of blond hair on his muscular arms.

"What did you say that address was?" he asked.

"Two-twenty-one Oceanview Terrace."

His head jerked. "That's the Rybeck house."

"Right," I said, remembering. Our rental agent had mentioned that the house we were renting had once been owned by the Rybeck family. "Why?"

"That house is haunted," the driver stated.

We looked at each other. "Haunted?"

He nodded. "It's a known fact on this island. An old woman died in that house. Her spirit is still there, or so they say. She's mostly been seen in one of the bedrooms on the second floor."

We didn't know how to respond to all that, so we kept quiet. Five minutes later we pulled up to the house. It was old and white and a lot bigger than I had expected. With a wary look at the house, the driver got out of the cab and pulled our suitcases out of the trunk.

Suddenly I had an idea.

"Hey, if I give you an extra tip," I began, "would you come inside and show us the bedroom that's supposedly haunted?"

The driver glared at me. I noticed that all the hairs on his arms were standing up.

"Buddy, you couldn't pay me a hundred bucks to set foot inside that house." He got into the cab and turned the ignition. "I hope you guys have a wonderful vacation."

❁   ❁   ❁

What you just read is from a ghost story I'm working on. Freaky stories (horror, ghost stories) represent a genre that guys love to read and write. All the regular elements of strong writing (vivid details, believable characters, suspense, voice) must be present in order to create a strong scary story, but there are some things you should pay particular attention to.

SMALL, DiSTURBiNG DETAiLS

Think about the blond hair standing up on the arms of that taxi driver. A visual detail like that clearly suggests the idea that something sinister is afoot. When a detail is expected and familiar (my sister's teddy bear on her pillow), it is reassuring. However, an unexpected detail (finding a lock of red hair on your sister's pillow) will instantly inject a sense of fear and terror into your story. Here's part of a story I've been working on:

> After the storm, I got up early and went down to the shore. As I expected, I found several wrecked boats, including one pretty big skiff that was lying sideways on a sandbar in the low tide. There was a lot of litter, plus two barrels and a big wooden box, which I realized was a

coffin. I moved closer until I was about fifteen feet away and stopped.

Slowly, the lid rose. A figure sat up in the box. At first he was looking away from me, toward the ocean. But now he moved his body around so he was facing me.

But the man had no face.

It's my hope that such a frightening image—a faceless man—will make the reader inwardly gasp or recoil in fear. If you've got an eerie detail like that, don't bury it in a paragraph. Consider pulling it out as I did, and giving it its own short paragraph so the reader won't miss it.

FiNDiNG TERROR iN THE ORDiNARY

But you don't need to have coffins with rising lids to write an effective ghost story. You don't have to go supernatural and invoke werewolves, ghouls, and ghosts to make things scary. I confess that I have a sneaky preference for ordinary stories about real things. To me, that's where the eeriest stories can be found. Look around your house or in places you know to find potential subjects to write about.

My mother-in-law was a nurse. Her old uniforms hung in a wardrobe in the attic. When my wife was a girl, sometimes as she and her friends were playing in the attic, a draft or slight breeze would reach those hanging uniforms, causing them to turn slightly. . . .

In many houses there are magnetic letters on the refrigerator. A skilled horror writer will take a commonplace detail like that and twist it for his own dark purposes. In *Bag of Bones*, an adult novel by Stephen King, the letters on the fridge spontaneously rearrange themselves to spell out disturbing warnings for the people in the house.

When I was in high school, I had a "friend" who delighted in scaring the bejeezus out of me. He had this strange plastic doll that was flattened, a half inch thick. The doll had brown hair and a smirky smile, and it freaked me out. This gave my friend a weapon to make my life miserable. To scare me, he would put it on (or in) my sleeping bag when we went camping. A doll like this could be very useful when writing a scary story.

CLICHÉS AGAIN

"In 1922 a storm blew Isaac Bumpus's boat to Quahog Island. They found the wreck, and they found some of his belongings on this island, but they never found his body. Legend has it that the spirit of Isaac Bumpus still walks on this island. Some people swear they have seen him, when the moon is _____."

Fill in the blank. If you guessed when the moon is *full*, you would probably be right. That's because full moons feature prominently in scary stories. In the last chapter we talked about avoiding clichés, but there are clichés in scary stories, too. These include

Vampires
Bats
Spiders
Cobwebs
Vampires
Creaking stairs
Full moons
Evil clowns
Disturbed nannies and/or babysitters
(Did I mention vampires?)

I'm not saying NEVER use any of these elements. I'm just saying that these things have been used and overused until they're just not that scary anymore. Why not take a fresh approach and look for the terror in new places? Let your imagination run wild. For instance, you know those automatic cleaners that are used in many in-ground pools? What if one somehow got possessed and turned evil during the middle of a pool party?

When you write a freaky story, you need to include some detail or event that is surprising, unexpected. In *Island Fever*, a novel I'm working on, Wade and his five-year-old sister, Molly, are on vacation with their family. They've found an injured crow and named him Russell. They are nursing the crow back to health. Take a peek at this section:

Just as I began climbing the deck stairs, I heard a small, clear voice. "Sam Terry."

Molly whirled around. She locked her eyes with mine. "What did you say?"

"Nothing."

"Sam Terry," the crow repeated. "Sam Terry."

"You talked!" Molly's eyes were huge. "You talked, Russell-boy! You talked!"

Suddenly she seemed to doubt herself. "He did talk, right, Wade?"

"He sure did," I admitted. "I heard it."

"Sam Terry," the crow declared. "Sam Terry."

A stab of fear hit me. It struck sharp and unexpected, momentarily blocking out the sound of Molly yammering beside me.

Molly grinned. "His name is Sam Terry, Wade! We gave him the wrong name! We gotta change his name to Sam Terry, okay?"

"I, uh, well, sure," I stammered. "Go pick some blueberries for Russell."

"You mean Sam Terry," she corrected me.

"Whatever. I'll go get the sunflower seeds."

She scampered across the lawn, exclaiming, "My crow can talk! My crow can talk!"

I went to the kitchen and lifted the bag of sunflower seeds from the cabinet. My hands were shaking, causing me to spill a bunch when I tried to pour them into a plastic bowl. I was glad Molly hadn't noticed how rattled I was. I took a few deep breaths, trying to calm myself and reconstruct what had just happened.

The crow's voice had been amazingly clear. Molly heard him say Sam Terry. But what I heard was a different word.

Cemetery.

R. L. Stine, author of a gazillion Goosebumps books, says, "You want to creep them [readers] out a little bit, but you don't *really* want to terrify them."

Perhaps, but then again, maybe you really *do* want to terrify your readers. If so, it's important to study other writers who do this well, because you can learn a lot from them.

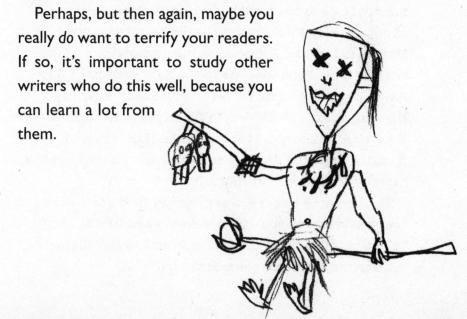

ROBERT SAN SOUCI

One of the masters of the scary story genre is Robert San Souci, award-winning author of the Dare to Be Scared series and many other spooky collections. San Souci has published 102 books, so this guy knows a little something about writing!

Ralph I always thought of you as specializing in fables and folklore. When did you decide to start writing scary stories?

ROBERT

I've been a fan of the horror genre for decades. Before getting into the scary story collections, I published several original paperback horror novels, including Emergence, about ghostly Pueblo ruins and a haunted church in New Mexico, and Blood Offerings, in which voodoo travels from New Orleans to the San Francisco Bay Area. My interest has always connected with my lifelong study of folklore, fable, myth, and legend. Emergence incorporates Pueblo Indian lore and Spanish legends; Blood Offerings culls a lot of voodoo history from the Deep South.

**   The books in Short & Shivery, my first series of scary stories for younger readers, each had at least thirty retellings of eerie tales from around the country and around the world.**

Ralph Do you think of the stories in Dare to Be Scared as horror, scary stories, ghost stories, what? How would you categorize this kind of writing?

ROBERT

I tend to think of them as horror tales (or, maybe, "horror lite"). They encompass all kinds of approaches to scares: ghostlore, weird creatures, haunted places, and so on. I've also heard this material referred to as "dark fantasy."

Ralph Did you jump into this new genre feet first? Or did you immerse yourself in reading other masters of horror? If so, who or what did you read?

ROBERT

Oh, I've been reading in the field as far back as I can remember. One of the earliest short stories in the field was W. W. Jacobs's "The Monkey's Paw," which I first read in seventh or eighth grade. My favorite novel, Shirley Jackson's The Haunting of Hill House, I discovered in my freshman year in high school. From these beginnings, it was a short hop to Bram Stoker's Dracula, Mary Shelley's Frankenstein, various collections of the writings of Edgar Allan Poe, H. P. Lovecraft, Richard Matheson, and, later, the early works of Stephen King, Dean Koontz, Graham Masterton, John Saul, Ramsey Campbell—plus countless others who have continued to thrill and delight me across the years.

Ralph You are very skilled at setting up eerie situations. What are the elements of a good scary story?

ROBERT

An eerie setting helps (though a story can be just as effectively scary in an everyday setting suddenly impinged on by strange forces of one sort or another). You need . . .

- **Believable characters who have distinctive speech patterns, quirks, and are usually sympathetic (though effective stories are often written about unpleasant or evil-leaning characters who get their comeuppance at the story's climax).**

- **Dialogue that rings true to a person's age and upbringing.**

- **Description of the setting and action that provides just the essentials a reader needs but doesn't go on endlessly. Selective use of details gives a reader focus and will often trigger the imagination.**

- **Ending the story on exactly the right note, at exactly the right moment, without then going on to explain what happened afterward. One of the stories from Dare to Be Scared, "The Caller," has consistently been singled out by middle-grade readers and up as one of the scariest in the first collection. I think that's partly because it ends at the moment "something" comes through the door into the girl's bedroom.**

Ralph In your story "Second Childhood" (*Triple-Dare to Be Scared*), a boy takes shelter in a crypt and stares at a coffin. You write, "Four thin white worms crept from underneath the lid, followed by a fifth, thicker one. *Maggots,* was Daniel's first thought." These worms turn out to be fingers. Great stuff! Are you thinking cinematically, trying to help the reader imagine it?

ROBERT I do tend to think in cinematic terms while writing. I usually imagine the story unfolding as a kind of "movie in the mind." That's probably the result of a lifetime spent watching horror flicks. I think selective details that draw the reader into the narrative and are just enough to get the imagination going are part of what makes a story particularly effective. I realize that any monster or creature I describe is not going to be nearly as scary as the horror readers can imagine, with just a few prods from details in the story.

This works in scary movies too—where *something* is barely glimpsed in the forest or around the bend of a tunnel. Often, when shown in full, these things can seem anticlimactic to audiences, who were enjoying having their imaginations and fear centers merely tweaked.

One of the best writers to use details to suggest things was Shirley Jackson (mentioned above). I've reread **The Haunting of Hill House** well over a dozen times and still find much to ponder (and shudder at).

My favorite classic scary story, W. W. Jacobs's "The Monkey's Paw," reaches its climax with the pounding on the front door, which is presumed to be the dead son returning because of the wish the wife/mother has made that their killed son return from the grave. Meanwhile the husband/father is horrified to think what might be on the other side of the door: an animated corpse, mangled in a freak accident, that's pulled itself out of the grave and returned. He wishes away the thing just at the moment the wife unlocks the door and pulls it open to reveal only an empty street lit by flickering gas lamps. By not telling too much, the reader's imagination can rev up to full tilt.

(**Ralph**) You have written dozens of scary stories. Where do you come up with your ideas?

I remind young readers that story ideas **ROBERT** are everywhere. I read constantly in the realms of history, folklore, legend, myths, ghostlore, and other paranormal events. I keep what I call a "Weird File" of newspaper clippings. The story "Red Rain" (in Dare to Be Scared 4) was inspired by a newspaper clipping about strange red rains that supposedly fell in India and other places that burned like acid and caused strange plant mutations. You just never know where ideas will come from.

The story "Fairy Godmother" (from the same Dare volume) was inspired by a painting that was used as an illustration in a children's book and was on display in the Brandywine Museum's collection of classic book illustrations. It showed an elaborately costumed "fairy godmother" holding a small child on her lap, while reading a book to him. But the child is gazing out at the onlooker, seemingly terrified, pleading. The "fairy godmother" has an almost otherworldly look that reminds one of science fiction's standby "alien gray." She also seems to have a sardonic, not pleasant grin. I arranged with the museum to get a small reproduction of the painting and—*voilà!*—another story was born.

The story about the creature in the wooded park grove that kids dare each other to run through was from a memory of growing up when, in the evening, we'd dare each other to run through a stand of trees at the edge of a playground, where undergrowth and shadows would, at times, suggest all sorts of creatures lurking. I remind aspiring young writers that their own experiences and memories can be great story-starter ideas. "Class Cootie" (a story in Double-Dare to Be Scared) comes from the cruel nickname and unkind treatment that one student received in elementary school.

Ralph I'm interested in your strategies for revealing emotion in a character without simply telling the reader, *He felt scared.*

ROBERT Sometimes it's easiest to show emotion by describing a character's actions rather than spelling something out. A character in an empty room, constantly drumming his/her fingers on a table, constantly walking to the window to gaze out, perhaps jumping at an unexpected sound, lets you know that the person is nervous, anxious, preoccupied, fearful even. How a person says something is revealing. "I'm not scared a bit," the character says, but his/her voice is high, or throat dry. Details like this reveal a much deeper strain of nervousness. Dialogue, of course, can directly reveal things too: "You're scared, aren't you?" she asked, with the hint of a smile. He said simply, trying for his own smile but failing, "I'm afraid I took the story about a madman on the loose a bit more seriously than you."

Ralph Do you use a notebook to jot down possible ideas?

ROBERT Yes, I'm always carrying a notebook. As I tell young hopefuls, nothing is more discouraging than failing to note something, getting home, and remembering you'd had an idea for a story earlier but can no longer quite recall what it was.

Ralph Could you say anything about creating tension/suspense in a horror story?

ROBERT We've already touched on some things: telling details, judicious use of descriptive words/phrases, keeping the action sustained without interruptions of unnecessary description, dialogue, and *pacing*—sensing just how much to reveal and how much to leave to the reader's imagination. The more you can engage the imagination, the more effective the story will become. Of course, an exciting plot, lots of action, and extreme life-or-death situations will necessarily engage the reader. Where possible, the sense of a mystery gradually unfolding will draw the reader along through a story, especially if the reader is made to wonder, What's really going on? I often borrow elements from science fiction or a classic British mystery story that serve the purpose of my horror tale.

Ralph I have noticed that many young writers think big—maybe *too* big—when they try this kind of writing. What I like about your stories is the way they deal with the ordinary. Could you say something about plausibility?

ROBERT I think what makes the stories in the Dare to Be Scared series or the new Are You Scared Yet? series is that so many of the settings seem "everyday." The kids go to the school just down the block, do gaming, chat on their cell phones, and go on family vacations. These familiar routine experiences suddenly veer into the horrific at some point. This lends an air of "this could really happen here, to us, to me." And that adds a layer of chills. The easier it is for a reader to identify with a situation, the easier it is to draw him/her into that "suspension of disbelief" so essential to the well-turned-out scary tale.

Draw First
and Write Later

When my son Adam was in sixth grade, he had a
teacher named Mrs. Reynolds who did nothing
but lecture. There were no
activities, no small-group work,
no getting up and moving
around the room—
nothing but Mrs. R talking
nonstop until the bell rang.
In order to keep himself
awake during class, Adam
would often pull out a
notebook and secretly
sketch. This worked
fine until the day Mrs.
Reynolds caught him.

"What are you
doing?" she demanded,

grabbing his notebook. "You're supposed to be paying attention."

"I am paying attention," Adam insisted. "Drawing helps me think and stay awake."

Mrs. Reynolds shook her head. "No drawing in class!"

I interviewed many boys like Adam who have gotten in trouble for drawing during class. Often this happens during writing time. Some teachers worry that boys draw in order to avoid writing. The truth is that many guys find drawing a useful entry point into writing.

"I feel more comfortable when I'm drawing than when I'm writing," says Renn, a sixth-grader in Hawaii. "When I'm writing I feel like I always have to add craft (that's what my teacher calls it). When I draw I always come up with short stories and more drawings. I get more ideas from my drawings. I draw to get inspired."

Recent brain research supports this idea. The human brain is divided into two different parts. With most people, the left side of the brain handles language (words). The right side of the brain thinks in patterns or pictures. (This is a little more complicated for lefties, who seem to use both sides of their brain interchangeably.) Many researchers have identified the right side of the brain as the preferred way of thinking for guys. If so, it makes sense that drawing can tap into the unique male way of thinking.

Ben Allen lives in Waterville, Maine. When he was around eight, he loved to draw elaborate pictures of the *Titanic* sinking in the ocean. Ben was a seventh-grader when I interviewed him.

Ralph: Can you explain your process? Do you typically write first and then draw? Or do you draw first?

Ben: When I was in fourth and fifth grade, I did a lot of drawing. I liked drawing baseball players like David Ortiz in action. As I would draw I'd think of a real game or a make-believe game and would soon start writing out the action.

Ralph: When you're drawing, what is going on in your head? What are you thinking about?

Ben: I'm thinking about the action of a baseball game and what the player might do, basically creating a game in my head and then getting it on paper.

Ralph: Does drawing help you picture what's happening in the story? Does it ever happen that while you are drawing you're thinking about what you'll write next?

Ben: Yes. It's like my own movie camera in my head. It brings the story alive to me.

Ralph: What does it feel like when you are drawing a picture? Does it feel different from writing sentences?

Ben: When I'm drawing, my ideas flow free. Writing has always been hard for me. Teachers have always complained about my handwriting and my spelling. Drawing seems like a safer and easier way to get my ideas out without being judged.

Ben's thoughts are typical of many boys I talked to. Drawing provides a comfort zone for getting the creative juices flowing. Recently I've noticed that some teachers have become more sympathetic to this idea and are more open to students drawing during writing time.

"I remember my frustration with a couple of my boys this past year who spent a lot of time drawing during writing workshop," one teacher admitted to me. "I worried that they weren't getting enough words on the paper and that drawing was just a way to avoid writing. It finally dawned on me that drawing allowed each of these boys to plan and organize their thinking. Each of them told elaborate stories to go with their drawings, and as the year progressed they wrote more and more words to go with their illustrations."

Let's take a look at drawing you can do that might make it easier to write.

DOODLiNG

Writers string together words. But strange as it may seem to adults, NOT using words at first can unlock the imagination for writing later. You can do this by making doodles, random shapes, or designs. Ben Whea, who goes to school in New York City, wrote a poem about this.

Doodles

Squiggles and spins
spins and squiggles
stray on my test.

I watch my teacher glimpse my paper,
zombies and three-eyed pigs soar through
straight blue lines.

She looks away with a sigh mixed with the lull of
eraser shavings raining to the floor. All that is
left is the hint of a doodle.

You might have to explain or demonstrate to your teacher that you aren't just fooling around when you're doodling, that this really is a helpful part of your writing process. Although doodling can be a great way to kick-start your imagination, it shouldn't be used as a Get-Out-of-Writing-Free card in school. Writers write. During a writing session, make sure you leave time to generate words.

SKETCHiNG YOUR MAiN CHARACTER

Making a quick drawing of a character can help you picture that character before you actually start writing words. Your sketch doesn't have to be completely fleshed out. Drawing can be a great way to become acquainted with him/her. Later, when you're ready to write, you'll find that you'll be better able to describe the character in your mind. When you sketch, make sure to include the most important features—muscles, hair, clothes, accessories (a cane or a purse), scars, weapons—details that will help define who he or she really is.

While sketching can be a helpful strategy, I do want to mention one limitation. Let's say you've gotten really good at drawing dragons or knights. Since those figures are so easy for you to draw, you might create stories about knights and dragons over and over. You can literally become trapped by your success at drawing one particular thing. Don't let that happen. Give yourself permission to write about a wide range of subjects, even the ones you may not be so great at drawing.

MAKiNG A MAP OF A SPECiAL PLACE

Look at the beginning of *Knots in My Yo-yo String* by Jerry Spinelli and you'll find a map of his neighborhood. (Spinelli even includes a legend with cool little symbols to mark important places.) I included a neighborhood map in my memoir *Marshfield Dreams: When I Was a Kid.* Making that map dredged up lots of memories I had forgotten, such as the time my brother shot an arrow straight overhead

and almost managed to get us killed when it came scream-
ing back down to earth!

Try making a map of a special place: the place where
you grew up, your grandparents' apartment, a summer
camp where you went on vacation. After you've drawn
your map, go back and mark these types of details:

- Power spots (mark with a *P* the places where kids gath-
  ered to hang out)
- Danger spots (mark with a *D*)
- Extreme stories (mark an *X* where something happened)
- Favorite places (mark with an *F*)
- Secret places (mark with an *S*)
- Unexplored places (mark with a *U*)

Each place you mark could provide a great idea for writing. You might be surprised to find that as you draw the
map, you'll start remembering things you had forgotten.

KEEPiNG A SKETCHBOOK
TO RECORD NOTiCiNGS

Leonardo da Vinci kept sketchbooks. In them he drew
what he saw with his own eyes, as well as images he
created from his imagination. Da Vinci sketched back in
the 1500s, but he was way ahead of his time: some of his
drawings predicted modern-day inventions such as the
parachute and the helicopter!

Many writers have found that sketching is a great way to pay closer attention to the world. I'm certainly no da Vinci, but I often sketch.

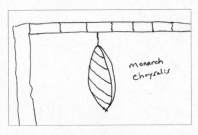

One time my kids found a butterfly chrysalis hanging under our deck. This seemed like a promising idea for a poem. I didn't want to forget what it looked like, so I made a quick sketch in my writer's notebook.

STORYBOARDING

Roger Essley, a children's book writer, uses a prewriting technique called "storyboarding," which is borrowed from the world of filmmaking. The idea is simple: you make blank boxes and sketch out your story before you write it. Start with six, nine, or twelve blank boxes on a page. The drawings should not be elaborate. In fact, they should be as simple as possible—stick figures are fine. The idea is to plan out your story with quick, informal drawings before you actually write it.

Dale, a middle-schooler, wanted to write about the time he went with a friend to a local airport and shot a BB gun at an airplane (a VERY bad idea). Until that time, Dale had been what teachers call a reluctant writer, a kid who always had trouble getting started. This time he decided to try sketching out his idea first.

It worked. After he created this storyboard, Dale found that writing the actual story was a breeze.

There are many other ways you might use drawing to feed your writing. (Some guys, for instance, love to draw political cartoons that make commentary—funny as well as serious—about the world.)

So don't exclude drawing from your life as a writer—invite it in! It's important to remember that words will produce the explosion that will make readers go *ooh* and *ahh* like they do at a fireworks display. But sketches, doodles, drawings, and storyboards can play an important role in the process, too, and really help to light the fuse.

an interview with

JARRETT KROSOCZKA

Jarrett Krosoczka is an author-illustrator who lives in western Massachusetts. He has written and illustrated many picture books, including *Punk Farm*, *Baghead*, and *Good Night, Monkey Boy*. He is also the creator of the wildly popular Lunch Lady series, humorous graphic novels in which the school lunch ladies are spies. Recently I caught up with Jarrett and asked him a few questions.

Ralph When you were in school did you ever get in trouble for doodling or drawing when you should have been doing something else?

JARRETT

I got in trouble a few times in high school because I was passing around my cartoons during class. I loved getting a laugh from my peers. Lucky for me, when I got caught, I was given the job as cartoonist for the school newspaper.

Ralph Could you explain your process? Do you write first and then draw? Or do you draw first? Or both?

JARRETT

Drawing and writing are so interconnected for me because I'm such a visual thinker. The way it tends to work for me is this—I get an idea, so I immediately open my sketchbook and draw the character. From there, I start making story notes in between my sketches. I attempt to map out the story (if inspiration is cooperating) by creating a story mountain (beginning, rising action, climax, falling action, resolution).

Next I make page after page of story notes, in the order I imagine them happening. Then I make thumbnails of all the pages I have to tell the story. (In a picture book, I tend to have thirty-two pages; in my Lunch Lady graphic novels, ninety-six pages.) I try to figure out what event will happen on what page. After that, I write a manuscript and then make rough pencil sketches of the illustrations.

Ralph While you're drawing what's going on in your head? What are you thinking about?

(laughing) I'm thinking, "Oh, man, I need to **JARRETT** meet this deadline!" Or I'm thinking, "Oh, man, it's almost dinnertime and I have so much more that I want to accomplish today!" Mostly I listen to music and radio shows, they take my mind away from impending deadlines and keep me focused and in my chair, working!

Ralph Does drawing help you picture what's happening in the story? Or, put another way, does it ever happen that while you are drawing you're thinking about what you will write next?

JARRETT

My books wouldn't be my books without the pictures, so yes. I'm always thinking about what my next story will be, but seldom when I'm drawing. Those thoughts happen when I least expect it or, more often than not, when I'm flying on an airplane. (There aren't many distractions when you are up in the air!)

(**Ralph**) So do you have some kind of sketchbook?

JARRETT

Yes, I keep dedicated sketchbooks to record all of my ideas. I keep all of my sketchbooks on a shelf in my studio. I have many of them, dating back to my teenage years. Once in a while, I'll thumb through them and find ideas I had completely forgotten about.

(**Ralph**) What does it feel like when you're drawing a picture? How does that feeling differ from when you are writing sentences?

JARRETT

I get so excited. Especially when it's a scene that I've been looking forward to illustrating. I tend to work on my art in the order that they appear in the books. So for instance, in the Lunch Lady books, the bulk of the action comes toward the end of the books. So as the action unfolds, I get more and more excited to illustrate the upcoming scenes. It parallels what the characters are going through.

✿ ✿ ✿

It's interesting to hear from a professional illustrator like Jarrett Krosoczka. You might not create comics or graphic novels like he does. Still, his ideas on keeping a sketch notebook, making a "story mountain," and doing initial sketches before the final ones are intriguing. They remind me that writing and drawing are very much inter-connected. And here's the best thing: Talking to Jarrett made me want to sit down and draw.

Emotional Writing Isn't Just for Girls

L ike many boys, my son Joseph rarely shows his feelings. Most days he goes around the house with the solemn "game face" he wears while playing goalie on his lacrosse team. At the end of this year's season, he and his teammates wanted to recognize the seniors on the team. The seniors had shown a lot of toughness and class, but most of them did not plan to play in college, so this was the end of the line for their lacrosse careers. To honor them, Joseph and some of the underclassmen had T-shirts made that said REMEMBER THE BROTHERHOOD. The jersey numbers of the seniors were printed on each of the shirts. It was an emotional moment when Joseph and his teammates presented those T-shirts to the seniors at the awards banquet.

Many guys act like we're unemotional creatures, which

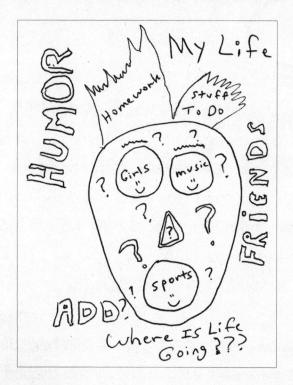

is deceptive. We may not always show it, but we definitely feel things and feel them deeply. And many guys find poems, stories, notebooks, and letters to be a great outlet for expressing those feelings. Not only that, but strong feelings can spark some terrific writing.

Our family lived in Paramus, New Jersey, for five years. My son Taylor was ten years old when we moved to New Hampshire. Taylor's best friend was a boy named Atif, who was really saddened by our move. A few months later he wrote this letter to Taylor. In it, he mentions his

Dear Taylor,

I am still your best friend, I just don't find the time to do these things, I get a lot of homework, I got sick for a week I had Broncrites with a cold and a virous and I was coughing alot. When I start writing a letter for you we have to go somewhere or clean my room, when I clean my room Junaid accedently throws the letter in the garbage, when I was sick my mothor wouldn't let me write a letter, when I go somewhere Junaid invites a friend over and they jump around and go crazy in my room, when I get back the letter is all torn.

Taylor to write this letter I had to stay up till 1:30 when everybody is sleeping.

P.S. I will never forget you

brother Junaid. There isn't a lot of mushy stuff, but the P.S. really says it all.

Writing is a great way to express love, sorrow, jealousy, and boredom, as well as anger. When my son Robert was in middle school, one of his language arts teachers spent an entire class analyzing Robert Frost's famous poem "The Road Not Taken." This infuriated Robert. In his Reading Response Log, he let his teacher know exactly how he felt.

> I HATE how you dissected that poem. That isn't what poetry is for. You took that poem and DESTROYED it for me! In my eyes it isn't even a poem anymore. Now that I "understand" the poem, it has lost all its mysteriousness. I think it's horrible for people to do what you just did to any poem. A poem is not just different sentences like you made it seem. It is one whole thing, like an antique watch. But now that poem feels like it's just a bunch of broken parts spread out on the table.

After the teacher read Robert's journal entry, she wrote back to him. She was surprised to hear that he felt that way and wanted him to know that she heard him. His words hit their mark. I admire Robert for being brave enough to be so honest, and I also admire his teacher for allowing him to do that.

❂   ❂   ❂

There is nothing sadder or more tragic than when someone close to you dies. But at the same time, a death can be the impetus for creating strong writing. Let's take a look at a powerful piece of writing by Jimmy Hernandez, a New York fifth-grader whose father was killed in El Salvador. More than anything else, I was struck by the heartfelt voice in this piece.

My Dad's Photograph
by Jimmy Hernandez

My Dad was killed by a guy out there in the world. The man killed more people, almost every one in my family. The man was found by the police the day after in El Salvador. In that country the justice system makes you die for the crime of murder, and he had to die for his crime the next day. But it didn't bring my Dad back or make me happy. My Dad isn't here to hug me, he isn't here to make me laugh, he isn't here to cheer me up or watch me get an award in soccer, which is one of my dreams.

I only have a picture of him burned, crumpled and smelling like a photo in the fire going away from its form to death. But at times I still feel like we are talking to each other. It's like we are using a phone from the earth's surface to heaven. I feel like I could touch him in my dreams. I know we will be together all the time no matter what! Imagine how great it would have been if he was watching me growing up. I wish I could hear his voice one more time. I wish I could meet him. I wish I could touch him. That's all I wish for.

In a strong piece of writing, you can feel an emotional current running through it. It encourages you to keep reading because those emotions make you care about the characters. I tried to do that in this piece I wrote about the last bittersweet day of camp:

When We Ruled the World

The last day of camp. The place is named Camp Harrington, but they should have called it Camp Bliss because we've had a blast. There are six of us—me, Sammy, Mull, Pedro, Greg ("The Slug"), and Trey—and we've become closer than brothers. But now it's over. *Terminado*, like Pedro would say. I know I won't see them again till next summer, and that's only if all six of us end up coming back to camp. A very iffy if.

We roll our sleeping bags and pack our stuff. Nobody talks. The parents can pick us up

anytime between nine and ten A.M., and we
are just sitting around doing nothing, when all of
a sudden Sammy, our fearless leader, leaps up
to rally the troops.

"C'mon, you losers, let's do one more loop
around the lake!"

So we jump on our bikes one final time, all six
of us wearing flip-flops instead of shoes, and start
pedaling like we're cranked on steroids. Sammy
is in the lead, singing the Coldplay tune that has
been *the* song of the summer: *I hear Jerusalem
bells a ringing. . . .*

He sings at the top of his lungs, like he's
some kind of rock god. We're goofing, laughing,
singing, swearing, flying round Kendall Lake,
when out of the blue a Volvo appears. The
Mullherns' car. The car window slides down.

"Time to go," Mr. Mullhern tells Mull.

"But, Dad—"

"C'mon. We've got a long ride back, and the
traffic's going to be murder."

Bang! Just like that, Mull's gone.

We wave good-bye to Mull, but keep riding.
Now it's only five of us. We are passing the stretch
of lake where we deliberately capsized our canoes
a week earlier, when a blue Ford truck appears.
Another direct hit: Pedro. His dad puts his bike in

the back of the truck. We can see Pedro waving *adios* from inside the truck as they drive away.

And that's how it goes during that last bike ride. We have no defenses. The parents pick us off one by one, shrinking our patrol, until pretty soon Sammy and I are the only ones left, pedaling around the back side of the lake. The road rises up and we reach the one place where we can see practically the entire lake sparkling before us. All of a sudden I can remember every single thing we've done this past month. The night we smuggled bags of Gummi bears and Swedish fish into our tent. The rainy afternoon we raided the neighboring Girl Scout camp. The "tube steaks" we ate and ate until they almost made us sick. The time we detonated a hornet's nest the size of a football hanging on a tree near the scoutmaster's tent.

Without warning, my eyes tear up. I swear I cannot see a single thing and have to skid to a stop so I don't crash into a tree. Sammy rides ahead while I stand there drying my eyes with the bottom of my T-shirt. Finally he stops and peers back at me curiously.

"What are you doing?"

"Got something in my eye," I lie.

He rides back and pulls up next to me.

"C'mon, genius," he says softly. "We gotta get back before our parents come. I don't want to be the last one left riding—and you don't, either."

"True."

"Hey!" Pointing across the lake, Sammy swears loudly.

"What?" I say.

"That's our car!" he cries. "We're under attack! They're coming to get me!"

"C'mon," I say, jumping on my bike. "I've got your back. We've got to make it back to base camp alive!"

❂ ❂ ❂

Feelings aren't just a girl thing. Emotions can be the strong, beating heart of whatever you're writing, but it's not simply a matter of letting it all hang out. There's definitely some craft involved in doing this well. Here are tips for creating strong emotional writing:

Focus on what's happening inside you (elation, jealousy, anxiety) as well as what's going on outside you.

You don't have to use the feeling word when you write about it. In fact, it's often better that you *don't* use it.

Include details that **demonstrate the emotion** instead of merely telling it. For instance: *In the doctor's office I counted every tiny square in the ceiling.* (Translation: I was bored beyond belief.)

Or: When it was finally time to come home from my aunt's house, I got dressed at five-thirty a.m. and waited outside on the porch even though my dad wasn't coming until eight. (Translation: I couldn't wait to get out of there.)

Think gesture. Often people reveal their feelings **more by what they do** than what they *say*. Maybe you're writing about apologizing to your father, and you want to show that you're feeling awkward or reluctant. You could describe yourself looking down at the rug, maybe kicking a stone on the street or hesitating before turning the doorknob to his office. Those gestures reveal your emotional state. If you **describe the right gesture,** you can trust that the reader will be able to jump to the emotion you are trying to show.

One last thing: When I want to share a strong feeling, I often turn to poetry. A poem is short and intense—a sprint rather than a leisurely run—which makes it perfect for communicating one powerful emotion. Here is a free verse poem of mine about how it feels to get dumped by a girl you really like. I compare it to channel surfing.

Changing Channels

It was like nothing
I'd seen at the movies.

You never sat me down
with a husk in your voice.

It happened BANG: like you
just changed channels.

Your warm Wednesday eyes
went cold on Thursday morn.

Would you please explain
exactly what has changed?

Keeping a Writer's Notebook

When my sons were young they each went through a stage when they became obsessed with making "traps." They found strategic places to build them, usually outside the house, using string, sticks, rope, or whatever random stuff they could scrounge up.

"What are you doing?" I asked Robert one morning. He was five at the time.

"Me and Josh are making traps," he explained.

"Traps for what?" I asked.

"To catch the bad guys," he said, dead serious.

I tried not to smile. I knew that if he and Josh ever did run into any bad guys, they'd get dropkicked into the next county, if they were lucky! But those boys certainly were dedicated. They'd spend hours perfecting them, peering around nervously lest the bad guys arrive before their traps were finished being built.

In a similar way a writer's notebook can work as a trap,

a place to snare and collect the raw material that will feed your writing. I'm a big believer in the writer's notebook. My writer's notebook is my bible. I have written several books on this subject, although my son Joseph likes to remind me, "You didn't invent the writer's notebook, Dad!"

True. Writers have been scribbling in notebooks for centuries. Strong writing must be fleshed out with ideas, facts, arguments, characters, plot twists, descriptions, and details. The notebook gives you a safe and private place for gathering that essential writing stuff.

A writer's notebook isn't complicated. It's really no more than a blank book that can be used any which way you choose. Some kids have been taught that the writer's notebook should be like a diary, a place to pour out your deepest feelings. While it certainly can work in that way, I'm going to suggest other ways to use it that may be better suited to guy writers.

CALLiNG ALL COLLECTiONS

We often have teenage boys coming in and out of our house. When I recently invited some of them to tell me about their collections, they mentioned bobbleheads, shed snakeskins, gyroscopes, stainless-steel ball bearings, Magic cards, Star Wars collectibles, sea glass, beer bottle caps, nails, weird-shaped rocks. . . . One boy confided that he collects bloody Band-Aids—*ugh!*

Guys are notorious collectors. You can extend this habit by using your notebook to collect whatever interests you, some of which just might end up in a finished piece of writing. That's what I do. I sometimes wonder if maybe I was a crow in a past life, because I love to collect various sparkly things I come across: cool words, believe-it-or-nots, unusual names (I once met a woman named Quality Sharp), weird quotes, odd facts. . . . My writer's notebook is the secret spot where I stash my loot. Below are some examples of how you can use your notebook as a place to collect.

ROCK LYRiCS AND RANDOM QUOTES

"I'd rather be hated for who I am, than loved for who I'm not." (Kurt Cobain)

"Excuse me while I kiss the sky." (Jimi Hendrix)

"A Jedi uses the Force for knowledge and defense, never for attack." (Frank Oz, as Yoda)

"Life is like an ice cream cone—you have to lick it one day at a time." (Charles M. Schulz, creator of *Peanuts*)

"One person's craziness is another person's reality." (Tim Burton)

"I won't eat any cereal that doesn't turn the milk purple." (Bill Watterson, creator of *Calvin and Hobbes*)

"When birds burp, it must taste like bugs." (Bill Watterson)

"Be the change you want to see in the world." (Gandhi)

"God is a concept by which we measure our pain." (John Lennon)

"No one's free. Even the birds are chained to the sky." (Bob Dylan)

"The main difference between your friends and your fans is with your fans you run out of things to talk about faster." (Derek Sanderson, hockey player)

I often jot in my notebook random or funny things I overhear people saying, for instance,

Fourth-grade boy joking with another boy as they get off the bus: "I'm going to take a picture of a butt and a picture of your face and morph them together!"

Mother at the supermarket talking to a very little boy: "No, you can't have a lollipop."
Little boy (starting to cry): "But Daddy let me have one lasterday!"

I talked to one boy who uses his notebook to collect lines of dialogue from his favorite movies, in this case *Tommy Boy*, starring Chris Farley and David Spade.

Tommy: Richard, does this suit make me look fat?
Richard: No, your face does.

Richard: Congratulations on completing college—it only took you seven years.
Tommy: Lots of people go to college for seven years.
Richard: Yeah, they're called DOCTORS.

I also like to stash obscure facts, trivia, oddities, and curiosities in my notebook. I do this partly because I might include such things in a future book, but mostly because these tidbits fascinate me. Here's a sampling:

• Mosquitoes actually drill two holes into your skin—one to inject a fluid into your body that will thin your blood, and another that sucks your blood into their body.

• The planet Saturn is so light it could float in water.

• The longest-burning fire on Earth is in southeastern Australia and is thought to have been started by a lightning strike two thousand years ago. It's still burning today, slowly eating away at a buried coal deposit.

• Most of the dust on your pillow comes from dried skin and the dust mites who eat your dried skin!

• Walkie-Talkie: My niece Laura spent two years in the Peace Corps in rural South Africa. She learned that the local people love to eat all kinds of meat, including some animal parts most Americans wouldn't touch. For instance, they eat the intestines of chickens. At the market you could buy a package known as "Walkie-Talkie," containing nothing but chicken heads and feet. It was very popular among the locals!

Some of my favorite acronyms:

- NIMBY—Not in my back yard
- PFA—People from away (used in rural Maine)
- PDA—Public display of affection
- AWOL—Absent without leave
- WAGS—Wives and girlfriends
- SCUBA—Self-contained underwater breathing apparatus
- PUSH—Pray until something happens

ARTiFACTS

I bet you'd be surprised to see what my notebook looks like. If you opened to some random page you would see words, sure enough, but you would also see relics and memorabilia from the real world including a Boston Red Sox game ticket, tickets from rock concerts, Chinese takeout menus with hilarious misspellings, clippings from newspapers, photographs, photocopies, candy wrappers, an invitation to a party, even a detention slip "earned" by one of my sons.

In this way, my notebook functions almost like a scrap-book. Many of the artifacts I collect are highly personal mementos connected to a special event, and each one can conjure up the original experience like nothing else. Being able to touch the actual Red Sox ticket, or the feather I found that day on the beach when I was walking with my grandfather, brings back a flood of potent memories and makes me feel like I'm there. Every one of these artifacts could be a "trigger" for a piece of writing.

APRIL IS
TSUNAMI AWARENESS MONTH
IN HAWAII

TSUNAMI SAFETY RULES FOR RESIDENTS & TOURISTS
Tsunamis are rare but they can happen

Prepare in Advance
• Look for the tsunami inundation maps in the white pages of the telephone book to determine if your residence is in a tsunami evacuation zone.
• Develop a family emergency plan and decide where to go during an evacuation. Find out where your nearest shelter is located.
• Prepare and emergency kit to last for at least 3 days. It should include medicines non-perishable food items, can opener, water, candles, matches, flashlights, radio, spare batteries, eyeglasses, personal hygiene items, clothing, copies of important papers such as insurance policies, family records, and property inventories, first aid kit, and bedding. Note: Pets are not allowed in shelters.

When a Warning is Sounded
• Listen to Civil Defense instructions on TV, radio, or NOAA Weather Radio.
• A Tsunami Watch means a tsunami is possible and you should get prepared.
• A Tsunami Warning is issued when a tsunami is imminent and you should move to high ground immediately.
• Wait for the official "all clear" before returning to low lying areas.

If the Ground Starts Shaking
• Go inland or to higher ground immediately! If you are near the coast and feel an earthquake, it could generate a tsunami within minutes. By whatever means possible—run, bike, drive—inland and uphill. If you are in or near a high rise building, go to a high floor.

For additional information, contact:
NOAA/NWS Pacific Tsunami Warning Center, 91-270 Ft. Weaver Road
Ewa Beach, HI 96706   **Phone: 808/689-8207**

http://www.pmel.noaa.gov/tsunami-hazard
http://www.nws.noaa.gov/pr/hq/itic.htm
http://www.co.honolulu.hi.us/ocda/tsunami2.htm

LiSTS AND SEED IDEAS

Selfishly, I'm always looking to collect stuff that could turn into a poem, story, or even book. To that end I make a lot of lists, jotting down ideas for poems, stories, nonfiction, novels. Once I've snared these ideas in my writer's notebook, I no longer have to worry I'll forget them. I love to invent titles for books I might want to write, even though I realize that most of these books will never get written.

- **Pumpkinstein**—a picture book about a giant pumpkin that comes to life, goes out trick-or-treating on Halloween, and terrorizes the neighborhood.

- **Stealing First Base** (it's the only base you can't steal).

- **ID Swap**—identical twins who secretly change places, not just for one day as a joke but permanently.

Making a list is one of the best ways I know to turn a vague idea into something concrete and real. Several of my published books started as lists in my writer's notebook. Take *Moving Day*. My family moved several times when I was a kid, so I know firsthand how emotional that experience can be. Since many kids go through it, I thought that moving might be a good theme for a poem collection, so I started listing poem ideas under two categories: Moving In and Moving Out. I tried not to censor myself, putting down anything and everything that popped into my head.

Poem Ideas — moving

1) Packing up
2) moving men — Hercules guys
3) Anger — I'm NOT MOVING!
4) Bubble wrap
5) Fragile (written on boxes)
6) Saying goodbye → best friend
7) Last night in the house
8) Goodbye party
9) moving Truck
10) Breaking a mirror → bad luck 7 years?
11) Empty house — echoes

Of course, not all these items turned into poems that appeared in the book. Later, I refined this list and selected only the best ideas. But the initial stage, where I cast a wide net for ideas, is an essential part of my process. This list eventually turned into my book *Moving Day*.

When my youngest son, Joseph, was in third grade I took him trick-or-treating. We saw a huge moon, a four-in-one package deal: Halloween moon, full moon, harvest moon, and blue moon. That night I started writing about it in my notebook:

> lunatic—lunar
>
> Neil Armstrong—first guy to walk on the moon
>
> If you walk under a full moon, you've got to wear moonscreen or else you'll get moonburned (hee hee).

Over the next six weeks, I gathered additional lines, thoughts, and images of the moon. Some were silly, some factual, and some poetic. In the end I had a dozen pages. Next I decided to write a picture book manuscript, selecting the strongest lines from my notebook. I didn't use everything. Those notebook pages eventually turned into my book *Hello, Harvest Moon*.

You could think of this process as going out for a baseball team. The scribblings I make in my notebook are the tryouts. The finished book represents the all-star team. Will, a sixth-grader, made two different lists and used them to generate writing ideas.

Top Eight Worst Events

8. Broken pinkie
7. Rode through French–Indian War battlefield reenactment (boring)
6. Left upstate New York and moved to Maine
5. Tuna (my pet cat) died
4. Penalty shots in soccer
3. Hockey tournament (3–2 loss against rival Senators)
2. Dresser fell on me and my brother
1. Got a shock from stereo

EIGHT FAVORITE HOBBIES

1. Hockey
2. Soccer
3. Making Lego creations—mostly cars
4. Teaching kids how to skate
5. Playing GameCube—*Mario Sunshine*
6. Taking my brother's stuff
7. Chasing my dog
8. My dog chasing me

GOOFiNG AROUND

Having a writer's notebook sounds like serious business, and it can be serious, but much of the time I'm just fooling around in there. I might make up wacky names for characters: a dog named J. P. Whifflesnout, for example. Maybe I'll freewrite, just putting down whatever comes to me without worrying about spelling or punctuation. One time I got the notion that I might write a book about imaginary insects: the spring-loaded scorpion, the math moth (with numbers on its wings), the meditating mantis (cousin to the praying mantis), and so on. I take my imagination off its leash so it can wander wherever it feels like going.

This chapter shows how some writers have used their notebooks. You could invent a whole different way of using yours: to sketch, record dreams, hide your secrets, copy snippets of strong writing you find in books you read. *Bottom line: There is no one way of keeping a writer's notebook.* A writer's notebook is a personal thing, so no two notebooks will look exactly alike, and no two writers will use it in quite the same way. If you write regularly in your notebook, say for a few months, you'll find a way that feels right to you.

So far we've focused mostly on the notebook as a place to collect stuff for your writing. But it has another benefit: Your notebook gives you a place where you can practice writing to your heart's content, where nobody will ever grade, judge, or critique what you write.

Author Don Murray, who was one of my important mentors, used to say, "I write for two hours a day, but it's what I do the other twenty-two hours that allows me to do that writing." Keeping a writer's notebook allows you to live like a writer even when you're not writing. It will get you in the habit of noticing, staying alert, collecting the fuel you'll need to run your "writing machine."

Read to Feed Your Writing

gathered with a crowd of people to watch a kite-surfer at the beach. It was mesmerizing the way he could maneuver that enormous kite (it must have been twenty feet long and ten feet wide) so it pulled him across the water. Suddenly the guy turned away from the shore and started skimming toward the breaking surf. When he hit a wave, the kite lifted him fifteen feet in the air before he floated gently back down to the water. The onlookers sighed in amazement.

I'm pretty sure that writing is a whole lot easier than kite-surfing, but both activities do have things in common. In both cases you learn by doing, through trial and error. No doubt that kite-surfer had had lots of spectacular wipeouts until he got really good at it. And one more thing both activities share: it's important to have a vision, an image of what it looks like, if you ever hope to do it well.

That's why reading is so important. It provides the crucial vision for your writing.

When I'm not writing—I'm reading. In the morning I read everything I can get my hands on, starting with the cereal box at breakfast, followed by the newspaper, then maybe a magazine. When I turn on my computer I check out Web articles and posts, blogs. Later in the day, after I've finished writing, you'll find me on the couch reading a novel.

Reading widens your horizons. There's no better way to develop your taste and get a clearer sense of what good writing looks and sounds like. Whenever I read, I discover an author using a new technique, new vocabulary, or a story structure I've never seen before or considered using in my own writing.

A few years ago I read *Into Thin Air*, the true account of a disastrous Mount Everest expedition in 1996. Jon Krakauer, the author, begins the story just as the climbers reach the summit, with ominous clouds rising up on the horizon, bringing the first flakes of what will be a lethal snowstorm. In the second chapter, Krakauer takes us back to the very beginning of the expedition. I never would have thought to structure a story like that—starting near the climax, then going back to the beginning—but it worked surprisingly well in Krakauer's book. Maybe I'll try it myself one day.

Equally important, reading will help you notice all the writing that *doesn't* work very well. Trust me: There's lots of badly written material floating around, and in some ways, it's as instructive as the high-quality stuff. Recently a friend recommended I read a popular YA novel, a book with a wildly imaginative premise. I got my hands on a copy and eagerly opened to the first page. Although the beginning didn't grab me, I told myself to be patient and keep reading. But thirty pages later I still felt . . . ungrabbed. The problem lay with the characters; they just didn't seem believable. The book did have a creative premise, but I didn't care enough about those characters to want to keep reading, so I abandoned the book.

Note to self: Describe your characters so they come alive. Otherwise, readers will wander off to other books (or the screen).

Often while reading I'll stumble onto a passage or sentence that blows me away. In a novel written by Graham Greene I found this description of an older man living in Africa: "The bags under his eyes were like pouches containing the smuggled memories from a disappointing life."

Wow! Right now

I can't write like that, but reading such a sentence shows me that it's possible. It inspires me, gives hope that maybe one day I can.

Writers read differently from other people. When I read, I'm interested not only in *what* the author writes about but also *how* he/she wrote it, in other words, all the decisions the author made along the way. Take this passage from *Touching Spirit Bear,* a terrific novel by Ben Mikaelsen. In this section the main character is weak from hunger. Cole manages to catch a mouse and eat it alive. (Warning: The excerpt is pretty graphic, so feel free to skip over this passage, if you'd prefer.)

> Cole felt the mouse squirming free, so quickly he brought his fist to his mouth. He pressed his hand against his lips and forced the struggling rodent between his teeth. It kept struggling, biting at Cole's lips and tongue.
>
> Cole bit down, too, and a tiny bone crunched. The mouse spasmed but kept squirming. Cole bit again but his jaw lacked strength. Still the mouse wiggled and twisted, frantically chewing at Cole's tongue. For a brief second, Cole felt a furry head pass between his back teeth and he willed his jaws together with every ounce of his strength he could gather. The small skull crushed, and then the mouse stiffed and quit squirming.

> With the dead mouse bunched in his cheek,
> Cole rested his jaw. Occasionally the tiny body
> twitched. Gradually, Cole worked his teeth
> together, gnawing on the body. Salty fluids filled
> his mouth, and he forced himself to again imag-
> ine a baby sparrow with an open beak. Food
> was energy, and energy was life.

I asked Ben Mikaelsen to talk about how he came to
write this remarkable passage.

"I included this event because it is very visceral and
uncomfortable for the reader," he told me. "In real life I
have never eaten a mouse, and never hope to, but I
thought it would allow a reader to realize how desperate
one can become. The reality of the scene came strictly
from my imagination. I guess this shows you how powerful one's imagination can be."

In Chris Crutcher's memoir, *King of the Mild Frontier*,
there's a hysterically funny story where one brother talks
the little brother into peeing on the heating grate located
on the living-room floor. John says . . .

> "Wanna do something neat?"
>   "Yeah, but just a sec. I gotta go to the bath-
> room."
>   "That's the neat thing," he says. "Go there." He

points to the four-by-five heat-register grate in
the middle of the living-room floor.

"Huh-*uh*," I say. "You'll tell."

"Promise I won't," he says. "Wait till you see
what happens. It's really neat."

By now I have to go so bad I'm dizzy, and only
my death grip is stopping me from peeing into
the wall like a strip miner.

"Just take down your pants and pee down the
grate," he says. "I promise I won't tell. I'd do it
myself, but I don't have to go."

"Have you ever done it before?"

"Lots of times," he says. "And see? I never got
in trouble for it."

"No, sir . . ."

"You'll be sorry if you don't. It's really neat."

"Okay, but you *promise* you won't tell."

He crosses his black heart.

In the same nanosecond my pee hits that hot
furnace, the yellow steam rolls up around me
like I'm Mandrake the Magician in the middle
of a disappearing act, which I'm not but *really*
wish I was. I know instantly from the *sssssssssss*
and the horrific stench that I better not be making
plans to play Roy Rogers again soon. I best be
rehearsing my role as a jailbird, because it's
going to be a long time before I leave my room.

This is a job for a bawlbaby. My eyes squint and my lips roll back over my buckteeth and not one tear comes out because every drop of water in me is shooting out like I'm trying to arc it across the Grand Canyon.

My brother calmly closes all the windows.

When the last drop sizzles off the top of the hot oil furnace, I stand, gazing dazed through the yellow mist. "You said you wouldn't tell."

"I won't," he says, "but what are you going to tell Jewell and Crutch when they come home and smell this?"

"You better open those windows."

"And let the whole neighborhood smell it? Then you'd *really* be in trouble."

John could always get me to help him pound those last few nails into my coffin for him. He not only got me, he got *me* to get me. I'm running around closing the rest of the windows for him so the neighbors won't form a mob to run my parents out of town for having me as a kid.

The very idea of a boy peeing on a hot heating grate has tremendous comic potential, and Chris Crutcher delivers. I love the dialogue, which shows the older brother manipulating the younger narrator. The vivid sensory details (the horrific stench, the yellow mist) make this scene hard to forget.

Writing Tip: *Rereading is just as important as reading. My writer friend Robert Cohen puts it like this: "I read everything twice, once to enjoy it, and once to steal everything I can from the writer."*

He isn't talking about literally stealing—plagiarism, after all, is a serious offense—but about going back a second time to notice all the techniques used by this author so you can try them in your own work. Robert Cohen is right.

When I'm reading I try to mark those sentences or paragraphs (with a Post-it note, a tab, or in the margins using very light pencil) where the writing is super strong. Later, I go back and reread those sections, often several times. I may even decide to copy a few sentences into my writer's notebook so I can refer to them again and again.

If you're seeking out great writing to study and imitate, look to published works created by professional word-smiths, but don't ignore writings by your classmates or friends. I've found a great deal of wonderful writing cre-ated by students. It may be unpublished, but some of it is as strong as anything found in the bookstore. Check out this piece written by Max Gilmore. There's so much to admire in it: the strong vocabulary, the skillful use of fragments, the questions in the first and final paragraphs to draw in the reader. This is a story about an obsession, which is always a fascinating subject.

Chocolate

Did you ever crave more chocolate than you can handle? Well, I did once at my twin little brothers' sixth birthday party, and it wasn't pretty. The culprit? A compelling chocolate fountain that my mom's friend had loaned us. The victim? Me.

After we melted the chunks of chocolate slowly in the fountain base and had got the "waterfall" of melted chocolate running like the instructions showed us, my mom put me in charge because I asked for the job. She was busy keeping the little kids from getting too wild in the house. Finally, I was able to play with the chocolate as much as I wanted. It was entertaining to see what I could make out of what seemed to be an infinite amount of CHOCOLATE! Also it was fun to share the chocolate with little kids and see how excited they were by it. Maybe their enthusiasm rubbed off on me. . . . Soon I was in the grips of a full-on chocolate frenzy.

Everything was great at first. So much chocolate. I was in hog heaven. I couldn't stop trying out new combinations of weirder and weirder stuff to dip in. Carrots, bread, apples, cheese, even a finger when I ran out of those! The best combination was the fresh strawberries dipped in the fountain. Mmmmm, I can taste it now. The scariest combination was when my friend Joe invented the "Spoonful of Hyper" dessert made with pure sugar dipped into the chocolate fountain. Of course, this is coming from a kid who puts about eight spoonfuls of sugar in his tea or coffee.

Then, gradually, I began to feel sick and shake all over. My stomach felt like an overinflated balloon that was about to pop! I felt miserable. Was there a lesson to be learned? Were my eyes bigger than my stomach? (First moral.) Yes, but I'd do it again in a heartbeat. Soon the sick feeling passed, but the joyful memories remained. And I guess I am lucky to have a fast metabolism. Isn't chocolate supposed to be good for you these days, anyway? My second moral: eat as much chocolate as possible at every opportunity.

So read, read, and read some more. Gary Paulsen advises, "Read like a wolf eats." Nothing feeds a writer's soul the way reading does. It will reveal a wealth of techniques, strategies, and new vocabulary you can use in your own work. It won't happen overnight but if you get in the habit of reading works by other authors, slowly but surely your own writing will get stronger. I guarantee it!

But it's more than that. Reading will turn you on to the raw power of writing. You'll see authors creating whole worlds, not from concrete, metal, and lumber—but out of words! That's the real magic of writing, one that doesn't require any spell or wand.

When my son Taylor was in ninth grade, he fell in love with the Wheel of Time series by Robert Jordan. He wrote this review of the series:

> Robert Jordan is a master. No, he's THE master. Never have I seen a book or series that is half as good as the Wheel of Time. Robert Jordan sucks you into these books, you become part of the story, you live and die with the characters, you lose sleep because you can't put the book down, and when you do sleep it's a sleep filled with the story Jordan has woken in your mind. Robert Jordan makes Tolkien look like a kindergartner writing his/her first book. He's ten times better, and that's the plain and simple truth. The only

> reason I give this book a ten is because eleven
> isn't an option.

I'm not sure I completely agree with Taylor (I'd pick Tolkien over Jordan), but that's not the point. What matters is that Robert Jordan's books turned Taylor on to the power of writing. Once you've put your hand on that live wire, once you've felt that electrical jolt, well, you'll never be the same again. And your writing won't be, either.

Nuts and Bolts

Practical Advice
for Guy Writers

How you write is as personal as how you get ready for school in the morning. Everybody's routine is slightly different; no two writers go about it in exactly the same way. Still, it's interesting to see how other guys tame the writing beast. And while there are no rigid rules for writing, there are a few universal principles that apply to just about everyone. This chapter explores basic moves you can make to write and have fun doing it.

RAW MATERIALS

To start you'll need something to write with: a pencil, pen, marker, paper, desktop computer, laptop, iPad. . . . When I'm home, I usually write at my computer. When I travel, I'm always scribbling in my writer's notebook. I prefer a fine-point Sharpie and a notebook that has lines, page numbers, and a hard cover. (I travel quite a bit so mine gets beat up pretty good.) There are other useful writing tools (pocket dictionary, thesaurus), but a pen and paper/notebook are all you really need.

A WRiTiNG PLACE

Most people have a "writing place" where they feel comfortable banging out words. It could be the couch near the wood stove in the den, the screen porch, or the easy chair you dragged into your bedroom. It could be your tree house, your parents' office when they're not home, or a corner booth at the local diner.

I have a "home place" and an "away place" for writing. My home place is my office. When I'm away from home, I love to write when I'm on an airplane; without interruptions from e-mail or text messages, I always get a lot done. I also love writing at coffeehouses. I don't want too much solitude; I like to have people around, but not people who know me. Oddly enough, the presence of strangers laughing and chatting with friends provides just the right amount of "white noise" that allows me to get lost in my writing.

Writing Tip: *The library can be a great spot for writing. It's a quiet place with lots of tables and chairs, and nobody will bother you.*

TiME

If you want to become a better writer, you have to invest time in doing it. Writers write. Period. Many people find it helps to schedule a regular time. I write mornings from about nine to twelve-thirty, the time of day when I feel fresh and rested. It may seem like having a set time to write goes against the idea of spontaneous inspiration; personally, I think inspiration is overrated. One of my favorite quotations is from the novelist Amos Oz: "I write when I'm inspired, and I see to it that I'm inspired every morning at nine a.m."

Having an hour or even longer to work on a writing project is ideal, but it's rare for people to have so much uninterrupted time. Most folks only have slices of time for writing: fifteen minutes before school, or the half hour while you're waiting at the doctor's office. Keeping a writer's notebook (see chapter 10) is a great way to take advantage of those small time fragments.

PREWRiTE WiTHOUT THE PAiN

I was at a young authors conference where writer Neil Gaiman gave a talk. After he finished speaking, one boy raised his hand.

"Do you plan out your writing before you write?" the boy asked. "Because our teacher says if we don't make a plan first then we're just winging it."

"I wing it," Gaiman admitted with a smile.

Rock on, Neil: I agree! I've found that elaborate outlines, webs, story maps, and graphic organizers are often more trouble than they're worth. What I do is simply start writing, and figure out the shape and substance of the story as I feel my way along.

So don't overdo the prewriting exercises, but don't ignore them altogether. If you're smart, you're writing even when you're not writing: thinking of ideas, planning, listening to dialogue, starting a list in your writer's notebook, paying attention to a setting that might enrich your story or whatever it is you're working on. Jotting a few notes is often a good way to jump-start your writing engine. And making a simple map or list to "chunk out" the parts of your story isn't the worst idea in the world.

TALK OUT YOUR THiNKiNG

Talking can be a great way of thinking through an idea, getting comfortable with your material, and climbing deeper inside what you intend to write. Find a friend or trusted adult and spend a few minutes talking about what you want to write and how you intend to write it. You might approach a parent or grandparent—sometimes even a dog with sympathetic eyes will do the trick! It's important that this person knows ahead of time what kind of help you're seeking. Chances are you want more of a sounding board, someone to listen, rather than lots of advice. As you talk, pay attention to what you say. If you do, you'll hear what sounds like the most important characters, events, surprises, details. Make sure to include all that good stuff when you stop talking and sit down to write.

GET A WRiTiNG FLOW

Think of writing as talking on paper. Imagine how you would tell your story to your best friend, and exactly how you'd tell it: "Okay, I had procrastinated long enough, and now it was time to go say hi to the new girl who just moved in next door. Trust me, I didn't want to—she seemed mega-dorky, if you want to know the truth—but what other choice did I really have?" The words you hear yourself speaking in your mind are pretty much the same words you would write on paper.

How much writing should you hope to produce at any one time? The answer to this question depends largely on how much time you have. If you have a lot of time, three-quarters of a page would be decent. I'd consider two hand-written pages to be a good session. My word processing program allows me to count words. If I can bang out 350 to 500 words, or thereabouts, I count it as a solid day's writing.

When you've got that nice writing flow going, don't worry too much about punctuation or spelling. Just get your ideas down on paper. You can edit your writing later. Oh, and one other thing . . .

DON'T SWEAT THE SLOPPY HANDWRiTiNG

Lots of guys suffer from bad handwriting. Because girls' fine-motor coordination kicks in earlier than guys' (by contrast, the large-motor coordination kicks in earlier for boys), their handwriting often looks a lot better than ours. Unfortunately, guys pay a high price for this because some teachers put more emphasis on what the writing looks like than on what it actually says.

I know what I'm talking about in this regard. I had THE WORLD'S WORST HANDWRITING when I was in school and, believe me, it's not a whole lot better now. But I survived, and you can, too. When you're ready to go public, or publish your work, you will probably want to make a clean copy. The keyboard really is a beautiful thing because you may have atrocious handwriting, but when you hit the R key, it always produces a perfect R.

Messy handwriting ("chicken scratching," my teachers called it) is something many guys just have to live with. If you can read it back, well, it's probably good enough. And on that note . . .

Reread Your Writing

Rereading your work is HUGE! You have to be the world's number one expert on what you're writing, and you do that by constantly rereading what you have written. I reread both while I'm in the middle of the writing as well as when I'm finished. As I reread, I ask myself various questions, including (in no particular order) these:

• Does this have a beginning, middle, and end?

• Does my beginning grab the reader?

• Does my ending work? Does it feel like a satisfying conclusion?

• Is it organized the way I want?

• In the places where I made a general statement, did I include an example or two to back it up?

• Have I described my characters so readers can picture them?

• Do my sentences sound short and choppy, or do they have a nice flow?

• Where does the writing work well, and sound how I want it to sound?

• Where does the writing not work so well? Where does it need some first aid (or major surgery)?

DON'T BANISH REVISION

A few years ago my son Joseph wanted to learn how to ollie on his skateboard. He couldn't do this trick, but he spent hours trying to figure it out. From the kitchen, I would hear him failing, falling, and cursing! Some days he came into the house with a bruise or bloody gash from a nasty fall. But he kept at it, practicing for countless hours, until one day he burst into the kitchen and announced, "I did it! Come watch!"

Revision doesn't have to be a four-letter word or a synonym for punishment. Joseph "revised" his skate-boarding skills until he could perform that trick. That dogged persistence or stick-to-itiveness (one of my all-time favorite words) is necessary if you want to get better at anything—including writing. If something matters to you, if it's important, you'll work on it until you get it right.

In school your teacher may seem obsessed with revi-sion. This creates instant conflict because most kids aren't interested in going back to revise a story; they would much rather just write a new one.

But don't ignore revision. It's an important part of what I do to strengthen what I'm writing. I may not be the world's greatest writer, but I'm a really good reviser. Here are a few tips:

Don't look at revision as a way to fix a "broken" piece of writing; rather, look at it as a way to honor a good one. By revising a piece of writing, you have a chance to turn a pretty good story into something really strong.

Let your rereading determine what you want to revise. Don't let the teacher or some other adult be the only one to tell you what to do. You need to step up and take charge.

Don't expect to revise everything. Often I write a piece that is sort of blah. Instead of revising it, I may decide to leave it and go on to write a new one.

Consider making a fresh start. When you revise, it may not be sufficient to merely tinker with a sentence. I often find that it works better if I put away what I've been working on, take out a blank piece of paper, and start anew.

POLiSH BEFORE YOU GO PUBLiC

I rarely worry about mechanics, grammar, or how to spell guerrilla (or is it gorilla?) when I'm doing private writing. But when I'm done, when I'm ready for my writing to go public and be read by somebody, I definitely want it to look clear and accurate. I don't want a spelling mistake or a left-out period to distract the reader from what I'm trying to say.

Reread your writing for spelling, capitalization, verb tense, yadda yadda yadda. . . . Your word processing program will check for spelling and certain grammar errors, but don't expect it to catch every error. My spell-checker didn't find any errors in the following sentence: "I don't except the argument that it's okay to altar the jeans of animals that have been bread for speed." But this sentence is completely wrong! What I wanted to say was this: "I don't accept the argument that it's okay to alter the genes of animals that have been bred for speed." So don't rely too much on the spell-checker.

A quick word about publishing. Writers have notoriously good imaginations, so you may envision that fame and riches will result from the book or stories you're working on. It could happen, but it probably won't. Christopher Paolini published *Eragon* when he was seventeen (actually it was self-published first by his parents). When Gordon Korman's first book came out, he was in seventh grade. But those guys are rare exceptions. My first book didn't get published until I was thirty-five years old. Be realistic and consider other, less splashy ways of sharing your work. If you're feeling entrepreneurial, you might make some copies of your story or poems, illustrate them, and sell them. Or give them as presents to friends and family.

FiNAL WORDS

The most important thing is to get in the zone and find a writing rhythm that works for you. Writers can be quirky creatures, sure enough, but most are also creatures of habit. It's important to establish the writer's habits while you're young because those habits will serve you well for a long time.

In school and out, kids feel so much pressure to conform, to fit in, to wear what everybody else is wearing, to make jokes other kids are making. That might be necessary for surviving in your social network, but it's not great advice for writing because you don't want to be some kind of drone-clone who sounds like everybody else. Rather, you want to develop your own unique voice. "Write about what makes you different," says author Sandra Cisneros. That's what will make your writing stand out.

Be brave and bold in what you choose to write about. Don Murray advised writers, "Do the writing only you want to do." If for some odd reason you're totally obsessed with drainpipes and want to write about them—go for it! It's amazing how often the best writing comes from the most unlikely subjects, as with this piece by Kenny, a fifth-grader in Virginia:

The Feeling of a Wedgie

I remember being wedgied by my cousin; it was my first one too. It was seriously painful, and a ride of a lifetime.

So I was playing video games at my cousin's house. We decided to play forts. I built a fort with the standard pillow and blanky set; Kevin armed with a pillow and a blanket; David (Sir Wedgie) had a blanket.

He struck Kevin, instantly stunning him, and dragged him into the blanket, then—"Ahhhhh!" Kevin had been wedgied.

I blasted David with pillow bombs. Unfortunately David survived my impact. Kevin threw his pillow at David. Kevin was rewedgied. Kevin was defeated. I was horrified; I was the lone survivor, and in a matter of seconds, I was wedgied.

It was very uncomfortable. I said I wasn't done yet and attacked David with a pillow. He wedgied me even harder. The wedgie left me numb. I couldn't feel a thing. I was sweating, and my bottom was on fire. But I kind of laughed at the feeling of it; it was painful but looking at my condition I couldn't help but laugh. Kevin said it was horrible, and I don't blame him. I was hypnotized into laughing! End result was a painful experience. I tried to be brave but in the end, I was defeated, perspiring, and tired, with my underwear rising above and beyond.

Kenny has chosen a somewhat . . . shall we say . . . peculiar topic to write about, but so what? This is a heckuva story, and you can tell that Kenny had a ball creating it. That's the thing: writing should be fun. Imagine riding a bike downhill, going fast, bumping up and down, just trying to hold on. Writing should feel like that. Write fast, write downhill, go with the flow. And learn to ignore the distractions that get in the way. So, fellow word-warriors, go forth and write!

SUGGESTED READiNG

2 Humor

The Princess Bride by William Goldman

Hoot by Carl Hiassen

Harris and Me by Gary Paulsen

Captain Underpants by Dav Pilkey

Guyku by Robert Raczka

Guys Read: Funny Business edited by Jon Scieszka

Knucklehead by Jon Scieszka

Invasion from Planet Dork (Melvin Beederman, Superhero)
    by Greg Trine

3 Riding the Vomit Comet

Grossology by Sylvia Branzei, illustrated by Jack Keely

100 Most Disgusting Things on the Planet by
    Anna Claybourne

"Squished Squirrel Poem" in *A Writing Kind of Day* by
    Ralph Fletcher

Touching Spirit Bear by Ben Mikaelsen

It's Disgusting and We Ate It by James Solheim, illustrated
    by Eric Brace

4 Writes of Blood, Battles, and Gore

The Graveyard Book by Neil Gaiman

Mossflower by Brian Jacques

The Gathering Storm by Robert Jordan
Guts by Gary Paulsen
Rats by Paul Zindel

5 Superheroes and Fantasy

"The Long Rain" by Ray Bradbury
Ender's Game by Orson Scott Card
The Sea of Trolls by Nancy Farmer
The Lightning Thief by Rick Riordan
The Hobbit and *The Lord of the Rings* by J. R. R.
   Tolkien
Dragon's Blood by Jane Yolen

6 Sports Writing

The Kid Who Only Hit Homers by Matt Christopher
Top of the Order by John Coy
"A Brief Moment in the Life of Angus Bethune" in
   Athletic Shorts by Chris Crutcher
Staying Fat for Sarah Byrnes by Chris Crutcher
The Contender and *Center Field* by Robert Lipsyte
Heat and *Travel Team* by Mike Lupica
Baseball in April by Gary Soto

7 Freaky Stories

The Haunting of Hill House by Shirley Jackson
"The Monkey's Paw" by W. W. Jacobs

The Collected Tales of Edgar Allan Poe
Dare to Be Scared by Robert San Souci

9 Draw First and Write Later

Diary of a Wimpy Kid by Jeff Kinney
Lunch Lady and the Bake Sale Bandit and *Monkey Boy to
   Lunch Lady: The Sketchbooks of Jarrett J. Krosoczka* by
   Jarrett J. Krosoczka
Wonderstruck by Brian Selznick
Knots in My Yo-yo String by Jerry Spinelli
My Life as a Book and *My Life as a Stuntboy* by Janet
   Tashjian
Robot Dreams and *Bake Sale* by Sara Varon

10 Keeping a Writer's Notebook

A Writer's Notebook by Ralph Fletcher
Amelia's Notebook by Marissa Moss

11 Read to Feed Your Writing

The Watsons Go to Birmingham—1963! by Christopher
   Paul Curtis
King of the Mild Frontier by Chris Crutcher
The Wheel of Time series by Robert Jordan
Swindle by Gordon Korman
Into Thin Air by Jon Krakauer
Freak the Mighty by Rodman Philbrick

Guys Write for Guys Read edited by Jon Scieszka

When Zachary Beaver Came to Town by Kimberly Willis
   Holt

The Devil's Arithmetic by Jane Yolen

ILLUSTRATiON CREDiTS

iv: Untitled, Robert Fletcher

2. Humor
9: Chubby-faced guy, Robert Fletcher
16: Great Guita, Robert Fletcher

3. Riding the Vomit Comet
20: Boogers, Adam Bissonette
28: Archer, Robert Fletcher

4. Writes of Blood, Battles, and Gore
33: Warrior, Joseph Fletcher
35: Sword fighters, Robert Fletcher
43: Warrior with shield, Joseph Fletcher

5. Superheroes and Fantasy
45: Flying SH man, Santiago Fletcher-Cursi
47: Poseidon's Warrior, Santiago Fletcher-Cursi
49: Beware the Robot, Francis Ohe

6. Sports Writing
61: Skateboarder on wings, Robert Fletcher

7. Freaky Stories
74: Night of the living dead, Joseph Fletcher
81: Witch doctor, Francis Ohe

8. Draw First and Write Later

9. Emotional Writing Isn't Just for Girls

11. Read to Feed Your Writing

12. Nuts and Bolts

INDEX